Becoming a Great Gospel Teacher

Becoming a Great Gospel Teacher

Bringing the Gospel Classroom to Life

ROB EATON

AND

MARK BEECHER

Covenant Communications, Inc.

Cover image *Luke Writing the Christmas Story* © Robert T. Barrett

Cover design copyrighted 2007 by Covenant Communications, Inc.

Published by Covenant Communications, Inc.
American Fork, Utah

Printed in the United States of America
First Printing: January 2007

11 10 09 08 07   10 9 8 7 6 5 4 3 2 1

ISBN 978-1-59811-256-6

TABLE OF CONTENTS

PREFACE

Rob Eaton
Rexburg, Idaho

I am a recovering attorney.

Actually, I'm one of the few ex-lawyers who quite enjoyed the practice of law. But in 2000, after years of prayerful pondering and questions about my sanity, I decided to leave the legal and corporate worlds to pursue a career in the Church Educational System (CES). Although I had found being an attorney and an executive enjoyable, I simply couldn't escape the feeling that I might be missing my calling in life. Two questions haunted me: If I could do anything in the world for a living, what would I do? and What would God have me do? I was truly blessed to learn that for me, the answer to both questions was the same: teach the gospel.

Coming to that conclusion was actually easier than making it a reality. In the process of getting hired and being mentored, however, I enjoyed what I quickly recognized as a tender mercy of the Lord: I landed in the seminary building of Mark Beecher.

I fear I am not as teachable as I ought to be. Perhaps because of this, the Lord sent me to be mentored by someone who was so good that it was obvious even to me that I had plenty to learn from him. (Mark is now a manager in CES Training Services, where he works with others to help improve the quality of teaching throughout CES.) During my training period, I made a concerted effort to learn all I could, and Mark obliged me by teaching me all he could.

Mark sat in my classroom every day and took copious notes. After each lesson, he constructively and candidly critiqued what I had done. Professionally, I have never been through anything so painful—or productive—in my life.

Once I was hired, I was doubly blessed to be able to work in the same building as Mark. We both taught seminary and institute students, and we frequently collaborated on our lessons. During that collaboration, I hope that I continued to improve as a gospel teacher. In any event, three years after joining CES, I was hired by BYU—Idaho to teach religion.

Although I have taught the gospel in various capacities most of my life, I have worked only a few years as a full-time teacher. Unlike Mark, who has worked as a full-time CES teacher and trainer of other teachers for many years, I write not from the perspective of a veteran CES instructor or religion professor, but from the perspective of someone who has recently been on the receiving end of some great instruction on how to become a much better teacher.

In this book, Mark and I share some insights into great gospel teaching, including lessons that I have recently learned in making the transition from the courtroom and boardroom to the gospel class-room. Our hope is that what we share here will help gospel teachers of all levels of experience, at all age levels, and in all contexts. All of us, whether serving as visiting teachers, priesthood leaders, Sunday School teachers, early-morning seminary teachers, or parents, are teachers in the Church. Elder Dallin H. Oaks emphasized the universal nature of gospel teaching:

> Every member of The Church of Jesus Christ of Latter-day Saints is, or will be, a teacher. Each of us has a vital interest in the content and effectiveness of gospel teaching. We want everyone to have great gospel teachers. . . . In the Lord's great plan of salvation there are no more important teachers than parents, who teach their children constantly by example and by precept. Each of us teaches those around us by example. Even children teach one another. Every missionary is a teacher. And every

leader is a teacher. As President Hinckley taught many years ago, "Effective teaching is the very essence of leadership in the Church."[1]

We believe the principles taught in this book apply to virtually all gospel teaching situations. While having knowledgeable students can certainly make teaching easier, great gospel teaching at any level requires considerable planning and conscientious effort. We hope teachers of all age groups, in both formal and informal settings, will benefit from the thoughts we share here. Some of the insights we've included in this book come from many years of teaching. In addition to sharing insights, we will often talk about the process of becoming a teacher in the Lord's kingdom. This isn't just a book of checklists or "to dos." Instead, we describe practices and principles to help the reader progress in *becoming* a teacher.

And while those new to the calling of teacher may be most hungry for advice, this book is not just for frazzled new teachers. We believe that even experienced teachers can benefit from the principles we discuss. The best teachers always realize they still have room to improve.

Whether you teach youth or adults, and whether you are new to teaching or more seasoned, we congratulate you on being the kind of teacher who is looking to improve. For your sake—and especially for your students' sakes—we pray that some of the ideas we offer here will help you better reach those you teach.

Mark Beecher
Saratoga Springs, Utah

Writing a book was not my idea. I am an introverted extrovert. While I'm comfortable in front of an audience and though the classroom feels like home, I often find it difficult to make good dinner conversation with another couple when I'm out with my wife. So the idea of writing a book just never seemed like something I could do. What do you say for 150 pages?

Then I met Rob Eaton. He's a gifted person with many talents, one of which is being able to diagnose problems and prescribe remedies. It must be part of the recovering attorney in him. As I watched him teach and shared some suggestions, he was a quick study and eager to try new things. It became a great learning opportunity for me as well as I tried to teach someone what I had learned through the school of experience. And Rob made me feel better than I ever was. As we talked and evaluated every day after seminary, he asked the right questions, and I tried to put into words some of the principles and skills that I had been blessed to gain. Each day became a "how to improve teaching" session—for me and for him. It's been a wonderful growing experience.

It's also important for you to know that neither one of us feels like he has arrived. I've recently been involved in producing a DVD for which our training division observed and filmed many teachers. None of those I interviewed felt like he or she had finally perfected teaching. In fact, the best teachers are those who are humble and teachable themselves. They often feel like they learn as much as their students. Writing this book has been that way for me.

Observing and dissecting teaching rather than being in the classroom the past couple of years has taught me something important. I've seen so many successes, and I've watched teachers change from the "sage on the stage" to the "guide on the side." Teachers who help others learn what they themselves have learned really bless their students. Rather than just imparting information, they help students learn how to become active participants in the learning process and take responsibility for their own learning. This is really what this book is about.

I must express appreciation to Rob for his perspective and drive to write this book. I'm grateful to the colleagues and mentors who have helped me along the way. I'm especially grateful to my wife for her encouragement and for always believing in me. Thanks also to Phil Reschke for encouraging the publication of this book with Covenant. And above all, I thank Heavenly Father for His guidance and goodness in letting me work in a profession that I look forward to each day.

ONE
NOT A BORN TEACHER

Some things just can't be learned. For example, no matter how much some of us work out and have the physics of jumping explained to us, we'll never be able to dunk a basketball. Whether it's singing, dancing, speaking, fixing things, or some other talent, some people just naturally perform certain functions better than the rest of us. We may even say someone is a naturally born athlete, musician, or mechanic.

Of course, plenty of other skills in life can be learned. Virtually all of us are reasonably proficient at something we've learned over time—like skiing, playing the piano, plumbing, or being parents. So at the outset of this book, we think it's important to address the questions lurking in the minds of many who have been called as gospel teachers. For example, can teaching really be learned? We tackle this topic, as well as topics in other chapters, by posing and answering a series of realistic questions and concerns of teachers we have met, ranging from struggling beginners to seasoned practitioners. So let's begin.

I'm just not sure that teaching is something that can be learned. I'm afraid it's like singing: either you're a born singer or you're not.

This is a legitimate concern, and it's important to get it on the table, because if we don't think we can improve as teachers, we won't try—and we won't improve. Far too many people in the Church seem to believe this, whether or not they think they're born teachers. Just as a belief that we can change and grow as individuals is essential to our spiritual progression, a belief that we've got the ability to improve as teachers is essential to our becoming better teachers.

And singing might not be a bad analogy here, although it's not perfect. As with teaching, some people are born with more natural singing talent than others. For example, one of our daughters has had a beautiful voice from the time she was a little girl. But we've also been astonished at how her vocal talents have blossomed with years of voice lessons and hours of daily practice. She can now do things with her voice she could never have dreamed of before.

With instruction, practice, and a dedicated desire to improve, any singer or athlete or teacher can get better. It's true that most of us don't have the potential to become a Pavarotti or a Michael Jordan, but we've got a lot more potential to improve than we might think.

Okay, maybe it's true that people born with some talent can build on that talent if they try. But some people are born tone deaf and will never really learn how to sing, no matter how hard they try. When it comes to teaching, I fear I was born tone deaf.

Here's where singing is an imperfect analogy, because you might be right about tone-deaf singers. The fact is that good gospel teaching really can be learned—with the help of the Lord—by anyone who puts his or her mind to it. Perhaps you'll never be the most remarkable teacher in the stake, but conscientious effort and good instruction can help even the worst naturally born non-teacher become surprisingly capable.

Rob's wife falls into the category of those who do not view themselves as natural leaders. Like many who are asked to teach in the Church, she dreads teaching adults and youth alike. Yet over the years she has studied the principles in this book and has attended every teacher training meeting she could. More importantly, she has diligently strived to incorporate the things she has learned. Recently, the stake Sunday School president visited her class and stunned her afterward by telling her she was one of the best teachers he had ever seen. She didn't believe him, of course, but she had to acknowledge that she must have improved considerably as a teacher.

Frankly, I'm at the other end of the spectrum. I've been teaching for years, and I feel pretty comfortable with my teaching skills—I always have. Sure, I'm not perfect, but at this point, I don't know that I can really improve all that much as a teacher.

If the notion that someone would articulate this objection seems a bit far-fetched, we assure you that the attitude giving rise to it is not. In fact, the objection is not that different from one that Rob once encountered as a zone leader on his mission.

Most missionaries who learn a foreign language struggle mightily to master the language—at first. But they eventually hit a point where they become reasonably fluent in the new language, and the sense of urgency disappears. They've hit a comfort zone, and they're not nearly as motivated to improve as they once were. Recognizing that some of the missionaries in his zone had hit this plateau, Rob challenged them to try to learn three new words a day.

One missionary who had been out just over a year protested confidently, "Elder Eaton, I took four years of German in high school, and we learned several thousand new words each year. There may be a few obscure German words I don't know yet, but I seriously doubt there are many useful words I haven't learned already."

He was serious. This missionary epitomized what Dilworth B. Parkinson, a professor of Asian and Near Eastern languages at BYU, called "returned missionary syndrome": "When a student becomes satisfied with what he knows, when he feels he 'knows the language,' he almost immediately ceases to make progress."[2]

Contrast such an example with Tiger Woods. He not only won his first major tournament as a professional golfer, but he won it by a record margin. After the celebratory dust had settled, Tiger sat down and watched the videotape of his tournament—not just to relish his victory, but to analyze his game. He was amazed to find a number of flaws in his swing—so many that he decided he needed to overhaul it completely. While he struggled to master his new swing, it set his game back a bit. But he finally got it, and when he did, he dominated the game even more than before.[3]

Those who are best in their chosen fields are usually not just those with God-given talents, but those who build on those talents through hard work. Doing that requires both humility and a drive to become better, even if we are already good, much as Abraham, already "a follower of righteousness," desired "to be one who possessed great knowledge, and to be a greater follower of righteousness, and to possess a greater knowledge" (Abraham 1:2).

But I'm comfortable teaching the way I teach. It seems like I'm better off just sticking with teaching the way I know how and not trying to be someone else.

We certainly don't advocate pretending to be something or someone you're not. And it is important to realize that we each have unique strengths as teachers. But if recognizing our natural strengths and weaknesses or personality types becomes a way to simply defend the status quo, then we are doomed to mediocrity. If we applied the logic behind this question to living the gospel, we would not experience any spiritual growth; we would simply stay on the same spiritual plateaus lest we try to be something we're not. In fact, we *should* strive to be something we're not: we should strive to be something better than we are. Recognizing and playing to our strengths should enable us to build on them, not rest on them. Just as becoming great disciples requires a steady upward course of change, becoming great teachers involves constantly trying to be better next week than we were today.

Elder Henry B. Eyring has discussed the need for us to raise our sights as gospel teachers, particularly as teachers of youth:

> The world in which young people live is changing rapidly. . . . The spiritual strength sufficient for our youth to stand firm just a few years ago will soon not be enough. . . . The youth are responsible for their own choices. But as faithful parents, teachers, leaders, and friends, we shore up the faith of young people. And we must raise our sights.[4]

As teachers, we combat the teachings and influence of the adversary. If we choose to coast in our fight against an enemy who seems to be continually gaining strength in the world, we will lose invaluable ground in the battle for souls.

I've tried making changes in my teaching before, but it's hard. It actually feels like things are worse than they were when I did them the old way.

Hang in there. We remember one volunteer seminary teacher who privately commented the following after an in-service meeting: "That stuff you taught us last time about how to begin class was great. But I tried it a couple of times and it just seemed too hard, so I went back to my regular way of beginning class."

The fact is that as teachers try to implement some of the principles we discuss in this book, they will find many of the new ways of teaching more difficult than their old ways of teaching. For example, when teachers who have been lecturing try to move to a style that involves more student participation, the first lesson or two can be painful. Just as golfers overhauling their swings might struggle, teachers overhauling their style might struggle. But those who patiently and persistently strive to improve the way they do things will find that the payoff in the long run is well worth some frustration in the short run.

Mark is "Exhibit A" in support of this argument. Several years ago, a new area director came to review his class. Up until that point, all of Mark's reviews had been quite positive. This administrator's review was also positive, but with a challenging twist. "You're a very good teacher," he said simply, "but you could be great."

Mark didn't know whether to be flattered or offended, but he took the bait. "What would it take for me to become a great teacher?" he asked. That question and the area director's response fundamentally changed the way Mark teaches. The area director told Mark that he was a captivating teacher but needed to have much more student participation (the subject of a later chapter). Five years later, when Rob first watched Mark teach, Mark involved students so well that Rob mistakenly assumed that Mark must have always been great at generating student participation. But the fact was that even though he was already a well-respected gospel teacher, Mark had overhauled his teaching approach and became an even better teacher.

It would take a miracle for me to realize that kind of improvement.

Probably. It certainly did for us, and it will for any teacher who hopes to become great. Fortunately, we're not just golfers trying to improve our scores through sheer practice, indomitable will, or clever insights. We are teachers of the gospel of Jesus Christ, commissioned to teach everlasting truths that can change lives. When we turn to the Lord for help, He magnifies and even transforms us.

When the Lord called Enoch to preach repentance, Enoch protested that he was "but a lad" and "slow of speech" (Moses 6:31). The Lord's response is a powerful promise that applies to today's gospel teachers with equal force: "Open thy mouth, and it shall be filled, and I will give thee utterance" (Moses 6:32; see also Exodus 4:10–12).

The bottom line is that whether we are struggling beginners or seasoned veterans, we must change if we are to realize our full potential as teachers. And with the Lord's help, we can.

- Any teacher can improve.
- Improving requires that teachers leave their comfort zones.
- Meaningful change usually requires both practice and patience, so don't give up.
- We can't improve all on our own, and we don't have to—the Lord will help us.

TWO

BE PREPARED

Almost all television shows about lawyers focus on what happens in the courtroom. In reality, most lawyers spend relatively little time in the courtroom. And when they do appear before a judge or jury, what matters much more than how clever they are in the courtroom is how well they have prepared outside the courtroom. Research and writing may not make great television, but they do make great lawyering.

Great teaching, too, begins with great preparation. In this chapter we explore why and how gospel teachers prepare outside the classroom for those critical minutes inside the classroom.

I understand that some teachers may need to spend plenty of time preparing. But I'm able to pull off some pretty good lessons without preparing, so why bother?

We hate to stereotype, but since we're men, we can slam our own gender: this is one of the most common mistakes male teachers in the Church make. First of all, most teachers who prepare their priesthood lesson during Sunday School and think they've pulled off a pretty good lesson have actually pulled off a fairly mediocre lesson. Second, even those few who can throw together a good lesson on the fly could present a much better lesson with preparation. It's that simple. Since our goal is to change lives rather than just pass the time, it's not enough to make it through the hour without a revolt. Doing the most we can with our time in the classroom requires that we do the most we can with our preparation time outside the classroom.

Is it possible to spend too much time preparing?

Sure. And as long as we're stereotyping, most of those who do spend too much time preparing are women. You have to be able to draw the line somewhere and move on. Otherwise you hit a point of diminishing returns, or overkill, and you're wasting valuable time. And unless you're very disciplined, preparing too much might actually make your lesson more difficult. Overprepared teachers learn so many interesting things that they almost invariably try to cram too much material into their lessons. Elder Oaks notes that today, "teachers can download bales of information on any subject." But the result of such research can be "stacks of supplementary material [that] impoverish rather than enrich, because they can blur students' focus on the assigned principles and draw them away from prayerfully seeking to apply those principles in their own lives."[5]

One other possible danger in preparing too much is that when we do, we sometimes find ourselves spending a disproportionate amount of time researching in sources other than the scriptures. The more time we spend researching our subjects in scholarly works, the more discipline it requires to focus our lessons on the principles at the heart of the scripture passages we're teaching—because we are so tempted to share all the scholarly background information we just learned. We're not suggesting that students of the gospel should never consult outside commentaries or books, since this is precisely one such book. But we agree with President Ezra Taft Benson that "there is no satis-factory substitute for the scriptures and the words of the living prophets. These should be your original sources. Read and ponder more what the Lord has said, and less about what others have written concerning what the Lord said."[6]

Okay, but I love reading about things like what course Lehi may have taken through the wilderness. What's wrong with that?

Nothing—as long as we keep it in check. We enjoy learning about those kinds of things ourselves. But we find that as we study some of the details and background of the scriptures, we have to be careful to keep our teaching focus on the most important aspects of the scriptures rather than on whatever interesting factoid we've learned recently. As we gain more peripheral knowledge about the scriptures, there's a real temptation to share that knowledge in class. Richard L. Anderson, an exceptional gospel scholar, once said that "it is an occupational hazard to be so technically proficient that only technicalities are of interest."[7]

If we don't watch ourselves, we'll discover that we've spent the whole hour talking about where Bountiful and Nahom might have been without discussing the doctrines and principles Nephi worked so hard to record. Nephi's own editorial policy makes it quite clear what he hoped we would gain from his work: "The fulness of mine intent is that I may persuade men to come unto the God of Abraham, and the God of Isaac, and the God of Jacob, and be saved" (1 Nephi 6:4). The bottom line is that as we teach the scriptures, we should remember that prophets like Nephi wrote their records with hopes of leading us to Christ, not to the land Bountiful.

But can't we use some of the deeper knowledge we gain about such things in applying gospel principles?

Certainly. For example, knowing that the borders of the Red Sea were a twelve- to forteen-day journey from Jerusalem, or that the territory was dangerous,[8] can help us better appreciate Nephi's faith in agreeing to return to Jerusalem to fetch the plates. That's a case where geographical knowledge can be used to underscore a spiritual point. But if the geographical knowledge becomes the end in itself, then we're missing the point. The bottom line is that, as Paul reminds us, the scriptures were inspired of God "for doctrine, for reproof, for correction, for instruction in righteousness"—to help us become perfect (2 Timothy 3:16–17). It's important, then, to teach the scriptures with that purpose in mind. Doing so can help us filter the kind of extra knowledge we introduce into our lessons.

So how much time should I spend preparing my lessons?

That will vary with each teacher's circumstances. For example, an early-morning seminary teacher simply can't spend the same amount of time preparing for a single lesson that a weekly Sunday School teacher can. But even with an early-morning seminary teacher, good lesson preparation requires more than just skimming the curriculum and reading the scriptures to be covered. If you really want to pin us down, a guideline that we use is to spend twice as much time preparing as you do teaching, at least the first time through the curriculum. But our general advice is that teachers invest enough time to prepare well—which we'll discuss more in this chapter. For most teachers, that means spending more time getting ready for class than they usually do. For a few others, it may actually mean cutting back on preparation time.

I've heard that it's better to prepare for a lesson several days in advance. But if I spend the same amount of time preparing, does it really matter whether I prepare a week in advance or an hour in advance?

Start preparing early so ideas can simmer. Let's say we're going to spend an hour and a half preparing a lesson. We'd much rather spend the majority of that time at least a day or two before we teach the lesson instead of the morning before we teach the lesson. The more time that passes between our initial cut at the lesson and when we finally teach the class, the more time we've got to mull things over and let ideas percolate. That percolating period gives teachers a chance to see or hear or read or experience something that triggers a prompting from the Spirit that they can use to improve their lessons. Some of the best lesson ideas come while teachers are mowing the lawn or driving—when we're almost subconsciously thinking about a lesson we have already prepared. Simmering is good.

Besides, once in a while teachers who let their preparation simmer will come up with an idea to do something out of the ordinary that will take extra time to put together. If you're looking ahead with your lessons, you can put together that PowerPoint or track down that crazy prop or find that old quote in plenty of time. But it's tough to do those kinds of things when you're preparing just before church. It's also great to have some time right before you teach to put the finishing touches on a lesson. But if you're still trying to figure out what you're going to do in the last ten minutes of class as you're heading out the door, your teaching will obviously be less effective.

Doesn't preparation get in the way of teaching by the Spirit? How can we say we plan to follow the Spirit if we show up with a detailed lesson plan?

If you completely write out your talk or fanatically stick to your lesson outline, then preparation can get in the way of inspiration. It's important that with all our preparation, we remain open to changing the course of the lesson based on students' comments and on promptings we receive during the lesson. As Elder Oaks put it, "If we slavishly tie ourselves to our own preparation or to someone else's wisdom or text—our teaching 'is not of God.'"⁹ For example, if the Savior had rigidly adhered to a previously prepared plan at all costs, we would not have the extraordinary teaching experience described in 3 Nephi 17.

But Elder Oaks has also noted that some people invoke the notion that they should teach by the Spirit "as an excuse for not preparing." Elder Oaks is not a fan of that approach:

> The Lord's instruction to teach by the Spirit does not relieve us in the slightest degree from the necessity of making personal preparation. Indeed, in view of the foregoing scriptures, the Lord has emphasized it. . . . We should be in constant general preparation by "treasuring up" in our minds the teachings of the gospel, and when invited to give a talk or to present a lesson, we should make specific preparations. Most of the time we will carry through with our preparations. But sometimes there will be an authentic impression to leave something out or to add something. We should make careful preparation, but we should not be exclusively bound to that preparation.¹⁰

So following the Spirit doesn't mean winging it. It means we prepare but that we also let the Spirit guide us, both in preparing and in delivering the lesson. Indeed, as Elder Oaks concludes, "Preparation is a prerequisite to teaching by the Spirit."¹¹

How do you follow the Spirit in preparing a lesson?

You follow the Spirit in preparing a lesson a lot like you follow the Spirit while teaching, but with more time and a little less pressure. We pray before preparing lessons, and then we listen for promptings of the Spirit about which principles to emphasize, which verses to underscore, which stories to tell, which questions to ask. The Lord knows who needs to hear what and which methods will work best with a particular class. That's why we pray for His guidance in shaping our lessons while we prepare, not just while we teach.

If I'm supposed to follow the curriculum, hasn't my lesson essentially been prepared for me already?

The manuals we get in the Church are a great resource, and teachers should definitely follow them. Of course, with our scripture-based courses, the scriptures themselves are the basic text. The manuals do a great job of focusing on some key principles and doctrines, but at least with the seminary manuals, teachers can't cover all the material for any one lesson in the allotted time any more than they could discuss every verse from the assigned block of scripture. The introductory material of the teacher resource manual even says that teachers should discover something on their own as they prepare to teach and that teachers are not required to use the teaching suggestions in the manual. The material is provided as a resource to be used as the needs of the students and the direction of the Spirit dictate.[12]

Of course, that doesn't stop some teachers from trying. And in trying to cover everything, they make sure that nothing gets covered well. That's why one of the keys to great lessons is to narrow breadth to allow for depth. When you teach with student participation and help students apply the doctrines to their lives, there's simply not enough time to cover the same amount of material you could if you just stood and preached or skimmed the surface of each principle. Breadth always comes at the expense of depth.

Focusing on two or three key doctrines rather than trying to cover every verse in every chapter may be the single greatest improvement some teachers can make in their teaching. Of course, there's so much wonderful material that choosing what to leave out can be very difficult. But we've learned that if we try to squeeze in too much, we lose the students. Instead of teaching a couple of principles well, we end up teaching several principles poorly. Elder Richard G. Scott emphasized this in a talk he gave to religious educators in the Church: "Remember, your highest priority is not to get through all the material if that means that it cannot be properly absorbed. Do what you are able to do with understanding. . . . Determine . . . what is of highest priority."[13]

When you're teaching Sunday School once a week, how on earth do you narrow down all the material to two or three verses?

We're talking about limiting a lesson to a couple of principles or doctrines, not verses. Take the Sermon on the Mount, for example. For 3 Nephi 12, we might choose something like, "Obedience is a matter of the heart." Under that heading, we'd talk about the difference between the law of Moses and the higher law, with its focus on intent, and we'd discuss the contrasting commandments in verses 21 through 44. We might also talk about how the Beatitudes aren't so much a "to do list" as a "to become list"; they deal more with changing our hearts than just changing our conduct. We've discovered that trying to bring our lessons to one or two points actually sharpens them and sometimes helps us find themes in chapters we otherwise would have overlooked.

So why not just publish a workbook with all the principles you emphasize from each chapter?

Because that would conflict with one of the other principles of preparation we've been talking about. Each teacher has different students and different skills and experiences. Two teachers could be perfectly in tune with the Spirit and come up with two completely different sets of principles for the same lesson. In fact, we often find ourselves revamping a perfectly good lesson plan we've used before— not because the first one was bad, but because the students in the next class have different needs.

Mark's work in the training division of CES has convinced him even more of the importance of this point. A training product that doesn't include a way for teachers to go through a process of change is incomplete. Lists of how tos or step-by-step instructions overlook the principles of agency and individuality. Good training presupposes that the trainer knows how to take teachers through a progression of personal growth that brings lasting change. This process is really the heart of learning a principle or skill. Similarly, teachers must go through a process of preparation when planning lessons that they hope will change their students' lives.

One of the things we like about the seminary manuals is that they give teachers several choices of principles or themes to teach for each lesson. We'll often add a couple of our own as we peruse the scripture passage for the lesson. Then we prayerfully winnow that list down to one or two basic principles we want students to learn that day— maybe three, tops. It's one of the most difficult and most important parts of a teacher's job. We'll also include some time in the class to cover larger parts of the lesson with summarizing techniques or other methods that give context to the lesson. It's important to do this without becoming unduly focused on details or story lines that would detract from what Elder Eyring calls "converting principles," which will affect the lives of the students.[14]

Sometimes I feel like I'm very well prepared, but the lesson still doesn't go well. I've got great material, but I just can't seem to get it to come to life for my class.

Sometimes teachers do such a great job of preparing *what* to teach that they leave no time to prepare *how* to teach it. It's great to decide that when teaching about Sodom and Gomorrah we're going to focus our lesson on two principles: making sure we don't pitch our tents toward Sodom like Lot did, and making sure we don't look back when fleeing sin. That's our *what*. But now we've got to decide *how* we're going to get those points across.

I'm not sure I follow.

Do you remember some of those guys in college who seemed to think all there was to getting married was deciding on the lucky bride-to-be? Sometimes the guy forgot that he had to convince the lucky bride that she wanted him to be her groom. Getting married involves more than just deciding whom to marry, although that is a critical part of the process. It also involves convincing that other person to marry you—which is often the more difficult task.

In that same way, finding a way to effectively communicate a message to students is often more challenging than deciding what message to get across. As teachers we are often tempted to just tell our students the message instead of figuring out the most effective way of presenting the material so they'll take the message to heart. But when we give in to this temptation, we have to remember that just blurting out the point of the lesson after reading several verses is about as effective as a college guy shouting across the cafeteria to the girl he's been dating, "Hey, you're supposed to be my wife!"

In short, great teachers spend almost as much time deciding *how* to teach a lesson as they spend deciding *what* to teach.

- Many teachers should spend more time preparing, because winging it doesn't cut it when we teach for the Lord.
- When you prepare thoroughly, guard against overloading your students with everything you learned.
- Start preparing early so ideas can simmer.
- Recognize that the Spirit can guide you not only in teaching, but also in preparing.
- Follow the Spirit in preparing and teaching lessons.
- Narrow breadth to allow for depth.
- Leave time to figure out not just what to teach, but also how to teach it.

THREE

IF YE RECEIVE NOT THE SPIRIT YE SHALL NOT TEACH

Business consultants are an extraordinary species. The best of them manage to learn their clients' industry and lingo in a remarkably short period of time. Seeing them in action led us to ask, "How would the best business consultants fare as gospel teachers?" What if the Church simply employed the best hired guns it could find to teach seminary and institute, for example? Actors, public relations spokespeople, and lawyers routinely and effectively represent individuals and causes with which they do not necessarily agree. How would they work in the gospel classroom? After all, they could probably master many of the teaching principles we discuss in this book.

The bottom line to this business proposition, of course, is that such spiritual mercenaries would ultimately fail. "If ye receive not the Spirit ye shall not teach," the Lord warned (D&C 42:14). That statement is both descriptive (no effective teaching will occur) and prescriptive (no teaching without the Spirit should be allowed to occur). Indeed, one good way to measure whether we are teaching with the Spirit is to ask ourselves after each class, "Could a great, unbelieving business consultant have taught that same lesson today?" If so, we have not taught with the Spirit. And according to the Lord, if we do not teach with the Spirit, we aren't really teaching.

Maybe you haven't been to a youth Sunday School class or early-morning seminary class. I understand that we should strive to teach with the Spirit, but how often can youth in a raucous Sunday School class or a sleepy 6:00 AM seminary class really feel the Spirit?

Some of our classroom circumstances can be challenging, but it's the adversary who wants teachers to lower their sights and believe that teaching with the Spirit can occur only on special occasions. Paul explained to the Corinthians that he taught in the power of the Spirit because the only way we can really know spiritual truths is through spiritual means (see 1 Corinthians 2:4–5, 13–14). So if we don't teach with the Spirit, our students may understand facts and figures, but they can't really gain spiritual knowledge.

That's why President Joseph Fielding Smith taught that manifestations from the Holy Ghost are even more effective than visitations from angels:

> A visitation of an angel, a tangible resurrected being, would not leave the impression and would not convince us and place within us that *something which we cannot get away from which we receive through a manifestation of the Holy Ghost.* Personal visitations might become dim as time goes on, but this guidance of the Holy Ghost is renewed and continued, day after day, year after year, if we live to be worthy of it.[15]

Teaching with the Spirit, then, is sort of like feeding our students spiritual oatmeal rather than what President John Taylor called "fried froth."[16] It sticks with them. Or in the words of President Smith, it's "something which we cannot get away from." When we teach the same material "some other way," our teaching "is not of God" (D&C 50:19–20).

So should I just call in sick if I don't think I can teach with the Spirit? Doesn't that verse in the Doctrine and Covenants really just mean that we won't be as effective if we don't teach with the Spirit?

Surely the Lord isn't telling us not to show up if we strive to teach with the Spirit but sometimes fail. But He is clearly establishing teaching with the Spirit as the standard for how we teach, not just some unattainable ideal. Here's how Elder Jeffrey R. Holland interprets the Lord's language in Doctrine and Covenants 42:14:

This teaches not just that you won't teach or that you can't teach or that it will be pretty shoddy teaching. No, it is stronger than that. It is the imperative form of the verb. "Ye *shall not* teach." Put a *thou* in there for *ye* and you have Mount Sinai language. This is a commandment. These are God's students, not yours, just like it is Christ's Church, not Peter's or Paul's or Joseph's or Brigham's.[17]

So how do I do it? When I show up to teach a Sunday School class as a substitute, the students won't come into my classroom from the foyer unless I call in the National Guard. I may have a well-organized lesson that I've put a lot of time into, but I'm never gonna move anybody to tears, except maybe tears of boredom.

Fortunately, tears aren't the goal. We're not necessarily looking for huge emotional breakthroughs or breakdowns. In fact, President Howard W. Hunter specifically warned against thinking you're not teaching with the Spirit unless students are crying:

> I think if we are not careful as professional teachers working in the classroom every day, we may begin to try to counterfeit the true influence of the Spirit of the Lord by unworthy and manipulative means. I get concerned when it appears that strong emotion or free-flowing tears are equated with the presence of the Spirit. . . . Let it come naturally and as it will, perhaps with the shedding of tears, but perhaps not.[18]

Teaching with the Spirit doesn't have to be flashy—just from the heart.

When Rob was a teenager, he had a few really good friends who weren't members, and they spent hours talking about the Church. But near the end of his senior year, Rob invited the friends over with the missionaries. At first, he didn't think it would be that big a deal because his friends already knew so much about our beliefs. But this night was different, because Rob opened up and bore his testimony, which he'd never really done before. Instead of explaining the gospel like a business consultant or lawyer could, he testified of it like only a believer could.

None of them joined the Church, but their reaction that night was different than it had ever been before. None of them cried, but they felt the Spirit.

That's why President Hinckley has taught that "we must . . . get our teachers to speak out of their hearts rather than out of their books, to communicate their love for the Lord and this precious work, and somehow it will catch fire in the hearts of those they teach."[19] Elder Bruce R. McConkie once said that when an inspired teacher testifies, that's when the "crowning, convincing, converting power of gospel teaching is manifest."[20] Perhaps the only thing better than having teachers testify is getting the students to testify.

You mean have a testimony meeting?

Not really. We'll talk more about this in a later chapter ("Testimonies without Microphones"), but students testify when they answer questions like, "How does remembering Christ's suffering help you want to live better?" They'll rarely start their answers with, "I'd like to bear my testimony," but when they share their heartfelt convictions of spiritual truths, that's exactly what they'll be doing. And not only will the class feel the Spirit, but especially the student who testifies will feel the Spirit and be taught by the Spirit.

So the first principle here is to testify and get students to testify?

Actually, it should be the second principle. The first principle is built right into Doctrine and Covenants 42:14: "The Spirit shall be given unto you by the prayer of faith." Sometimes when we look back on a lesson that felt flat, we realize that we didn't really take the time to plead with Heavenly Father for direction in preparing our lesson or for the help of the Spirit in giving it. On the other hand, when we plead with the Lord, the Spirit is almost always there when we teach.

Almost?

There's always agency. As we'll discuss more in the next chapter, sometimes despite our best efforts, students simply aren't prepared or willing to let the Spirit into their hearts. Nephi acknowledged that when a person speaks by the power of the Holy Ghost, "the Holy Ghost carrieth it *unto* the hearts of the children of men"—but not *into* their hearts (2 Nephi 33:1; emphasis added). We can't force anyone to feel the Spirit, but we can do everything in our power to increase the odds that we actually communicate with our students through the Spirit.

Okay, so what else can I do to teach with the Spirit besides pray with faith and testify?

Virtually all the principles we discuss in this book can contribute to teaching with the Spirit. But one that warrants particular mention here is loving the students and remembering that we're teaching students, not lessons. We find that if we're simply trying to cover material because we need to get through a lesson, we're less likely to be teaching with the Spirit.

Once, when teaching the plan of salvation at the beginning of the seminary year, we decided that a great way to bring home the doctrines to the students would be to have them do the teaching—to someone who was not a member. We managed to find a few good sports in our wards who were married to members but weren't members themselves. Students in one of the first classes to do this experiment were understandably nervous, and their main concern seemed to be just covering their lesson's points. Later classes focused more on making sure they really got through to the person they were teaching; they were more concerned about teaching the person than covering the material. You could feel much more of a connection between those students and the "investigator," and that connection facilitated the flow of the Spirit.

This is exactly what Elder Dallin H. Oaks was talking about when he said,

> A gospel teacher, like the Master we serve, will concentrate entirely on those being taught. His or her total concentration will be on the needs of the sheep—the good of the students. A gospel teacher does not focus on himself or herself. One who understands that principle will not look upon his or her calling as "giving or presenting a lesson," because that definition views teaching from the standpoint of the teacher, not the student.[21]

Remembering that we're teaching students rather than lessons helps not only in executing lessons, but in preparing them. Sometimes as we prepare, we pray and try to visualize one particular student. We'll shape the lesson with him or her in mind.

When Rob was interviewing to teach at BYU—Idaho, he had an interesting experience with this concept. He worked very hard to prepare the lesson he would teach to a class of students in front of the hiring committee. Just a couple of days before teaching the class, Rob realized that his preparation was all about him, not his students. He was worrying about how he'd look to the committee, not about teaching individual students what they needed to hear.

So Rob stopped praying for himself and began praying that if some student in class that day needed to hear something in particular, he would be prompted to say it or ask a question that would lead someone else to say it. After Rob finished teaching that day, a young woman came up to him visibly moved. She said that she'd really been struggling with something, but that day in class she'd heard just what she needed to hear. In that moment, Rob knew the most important thing that had happened that day was that this young woman had been taught by the Spirit.

So I need to seek the Spirit by praying with faith, testifying, and learning to love the students. What else?

Perhaps this should go without saying, but teachers must also live the gospel. This is one of the biggest reasons that consultants or actors could never teach the gospel as effectively as humble, struggling teachers who are doing their best to live the gospel. No matter how well they understood the concepts or how articulate they were, any encouragement they gave to live a certain way would feel rather hollow if they weren't really striving to practice what they preached. It's pretty difficult to testify about the importance of keeping the Sabbath holy or writing in your journal or forgiving others if you're not really trying to do those things yourself. President Harold B. Lee taught, "You cannot light a fire in another soul unless it is burning in your own soul."[22] That's why, as President Benson said, "your first responsibility as a teacher of the gospel is to prepare yourself spiritually."[23]

None of us is perfect, but when we're really trying to live the gospel, it makes a big difference in our ability to teach gospel principles with the power of the Spirit. And while teachers need to be careful not to be self-promoting, some of the best spiritual experiences in any classroom come when the teacher shares a personal experience about how living the gospel has blessed his or her life.

With that in mind, one of the great challenges to teaching the gospel every day is that it almost forces conscientious teachers to resolve their disputes and keep things in order in their lives. It's difficult to have an ongoing spat with your spouse and teach with the Spirit. Joseph Smith experienced that same principle when translating the Book of Mormon. According to David Whitmer, Joseph came up to translate one afternoon after he and Emma had a disagreement. Joseph tried to resume translating but couldn't—the Spirit wouldn't flow. Finally, Joseph excused himself to pray and patch things up with Emma. He then was able to resume translating.[24] It's a great example of how teachers really need to be living worthily and peacefully if they hope to teach with the Spirit.

Besides living the gospel and avoiding arguments with my spouse, are there any other keys that you have found to be particularly effective in inviting the Spirit into the classroom?

Make a direct invitation. As part of Mark's current job in CES training, he has observed and filmed many teachers. He has watched teachers prompt students with a simple invitation, such as, "As you read the next few verses on your own, pay attention to your thoughts and feelings. Note words or phrases that the Spirit seems to highlight for you." Other teachers gave an invitation like this: "As we study our scriptures today, be sure to have a red pencil handy. Underline those things that the Spirit is bringing to light for you. Doctrine and Covenants 8:2 says that revelation comes to our heart and mind. Try to see how that will work for you today." Helping students focus on the Spirit will often invite a more spiritual feeling into a classroom.

Music is another great way to invite the Spirit into a classroom. At first we were bashful about using music in class. But we have discovered that few things facilitate the flow of the Spirit like music. We scour the hymnbook, the Primary songbook, Especially for Youth CDs, and Mormon Tabernacle Choir CDs for powerful hymns and songs that convey the principles we're teaching. For example, there's nothing quite like "Come Thou Fount of Every Blessing" to drive home how much we need grace in our lives. "When I Survey the Wondrous Cross" and "I Stand All Amazed" do wonders in helping teach about gratitude for the Atonement. Primary songs even work with teenagers. In fact, some of our best opening hymns we've had have been the male/female duets from the *Children's Songbook*. Even with college students at BYU—Idaho, Rob often plays appropriate music while having students ponder particular questions relating to the scriptural principles they are studying. One of Mark's highlights was teaching sections 109 and 110 of the Doctrine and Covenants. Learning and feeling the significance of the sacred events that took place in the Kirtland Temple was a spiritual experience. But singing "The Spirit of God" with a group of teenagers created an even more realistic feeling of what it meant to "sing and . . . shout with the armies of heaven, Hosanna, hosanna to God and the Lamb" (*Hymns,* no. 2).

I'm afraid it's going to take a miracle for me to teach with the Spirit.

Yes, it will. In fact, that's an important realization. When we think we can carry the class all by ourselves through hard work, clever object lessons, profound insights, or funny personal stories, that's when we get into trouble. But when we plead with the Lord for the miracle of teaching by the Spirit, He blesses us. Of course, we need to do our part as well—and that includes things like praying with faith, testifying and teaching from the heart, loving the students, living the gospel, making direct invitations, and using music. But ultimately, it is the Lord who will send the Spirit to really take the gospel into the hearts of receptive students. Like Ammon, we seek to become His instruments (see Alma 17:11), but God is the conductor. Our students are His children. He will lead them home.

- Pray for the Spirit.
- Testify—and get students to testify.
- Teach with love, focusing on teaching students instead of lessons.
- Prepare spiritually.
- Invite students to recognize promptings of the Spirit.
- Use music to facilitate the flow of the Spirit.

FOUR

SHIFTING THE BURDEN

Teaching with the Spirit is to gospel learning as flour is to cinnamon rolls: it's an absolutely necessary ingredient—but it is only part of the recipe. In a 2006 talk to religious educators that will probably influence gospel teaching for years to come, Elder David A. Bednar reminded us of another critical ingredient that is often overlooked in the recipe for learning gospel truths: learning by faith.[25]

As a seminary teacher, Elder Jay E. Jensen received "one of the most valuable lessons [he] ever learned" from a supervisor who understood this principle well. The supervisor made this simple suggestion after watching Brother Jensen teach: "Learn to put more of the burden of the learning on the student. You assume too much of it. Shift it." That advice has remained with Elder Jensen through the years, as evidenced by his plea to BYU—Idaho teachers in 2005: "We have got to do more both ecclesiastically and educationally in helping people become learners—to become better learners."[26]

When we teach by the Spirit, we knock on the door of students' hearts (see 2 Nephi 33:1), but they must open the door to the Spirit if real learning is to occur. "Ultimately . . . the content of a message and the witness of the Holy Ghost penetrate into the heart only if a receiver allows them to enter," Elder Bednar notes.[27] That's why he calls preaching by the Spirit and learning by faith "companion principles that we should strive to understand and apply concurrently and consistently."[28] This companion principle of learning by faith is critical, according to Elder Bednar, because "learning by faith cannot be transferred from an instructor to a student through a lecture, a demonstration, or an experiential exercise; rather, a student must exercise faith and act in order to obtain the knowledge for himself or herself."[29] In short, if our students fail to act, they'll fail to learn, despite our best efforts to teach by the Spirit.

In this chapter, we don't attempt to describe all the ways in which we can and should learn by faith. Instead, we focus on what teachers can do to help their students exercise their agency to learn by faith.

Why even bother to mention learning by faith in a book on gospel teaching, if learning by faith is the students' responsibility, not mine?

Because understanding this fact should fundamentally change the way we teach.

How?

Rather than just fulfilling their responsibility to teach with the Spirit, great gospel teachers strive to help students understand and fulfill their responsibility to learn by the Spirit. In fact, according to Elder Bednar, "We are most effective as instructors when we encourage and facilitate learning by faith."[30] Teachers who give students insights teach them for a day; teachers who show students how to discover insights for themselves teach them for a lifetime. That's why Virginia H. Pearce suggested that "a skilled teacher doesn't think, 'What shall I do in class today?' but asks, 'What will my students do in class today?'; not, 'What will I teach today?' but rather, 'How will I help my students discover what they need to know?'"[31]

As teachers, then, we should remember that, in the words of Elder Bednar, "The most important learnings of life are caught—not taught."[32] Rob witnessed Elder Bednar apply this principle during a question-and-answer session at BYU—Idaho in 2005, when a student asked Elder Bednar the reference for a scripture he had quoted. "If I tell you, you'll never remember," Elder Bednar replied. "If you discover it for yourself, you'll never forget."[33]

And the research shows Elder Bednar is right: students retain insights much better when they participate in discovering them.[34] The same thing happens when we give students the opportunity to articulate and apply gospel truths in a classroom setting. Such experiences, observes Elder Scott, "will anchor truths in their minds and hearts."[35] This is exactly the kind of thing Elder Jensen's supervisor was talking about when he urged Elder Jensen to shift the burden.

So just how do we shift the burden? By refusing to answer their questions? By only having them talk in class?

Student participation and teacher restraint—in appropriate circumstances—are part of how we shift the burden. But for a lot of gospel teachers and students, this approach is completely different from what they're used to, which is mostly lecturing. President Harold B. Lee once "expressed his deep concern about the fact that some [students] could go through Primary, Sunday School, Mutual, priesthood quorums, and seminary and come out the other end without testimonies." His explanation for why this was happening was simple: *"Because our young people have grown up spectators."*[36]

Mark recently trained a group of curriculum writers. In the training he used the analogy of baking. He brought doughnuts, muffins, and bagels to the meeting. After the writers had selected their treats and settled into their chairs, Mark talked about all the tasty lessons that teachers produce. For years, teachers have been using similar ingredients such as flour, eggs, sugar, and oil to produce teaching treats for their students. In addition, good teachers have focused on serving it with elegance and style. But what we're asking teachers to do now is very different. As important as it is to decide what to serve and how to serve it, there is another important question to answer: who's making the dough? Teachers can't just think that getting students to participate is a new variety of baking a lesson. It's a fundamental shift. Teachers can teach all kinds of creative lessons that are wonderful and memorable. But in these last days, it's vital that students learn how to make the dough so that they can make the baked goods in their own lives and for their families. It's the proverbial difference between catching fish for students and teaching them to fish. "As gospel instructors," Elder Bednar reminds us, "you and I are not in the business of distributing fish; rather, our work is to help individuals learn to 'fish' and to become spiritually self-reliant."[37]

Getting students to become participants instead of just spectators might require us to help them understand the reasons for this different approach to learning. It's almost like the shift King Mosiah asked his people to make from a monarchy—where the king had all the answers—to a more democratic form of government. After he explained to the people how great the load was on the king, Mosiah explained that "the burden should come upon all the people, that every man might bear his part" (Mosiah 29:34). Two verses later we read that the people gave up their desire for a king—remember it took some persuading for the people to be willing to make this change— and pretty soon they even became eager "that every man should have an equal chance throughout all the land; yea, and every man expressed a willingness to answer for his own sins" (Mosiah 29:38).

That's the kind of change that needs to occur in a lot of class-rooms—from a benign dictatorship, where the teacher lectures or entertains and spoon-feeds truths to students, to a more participatory environment, where students share in the responsibility to learn for themselves. In fact, it's interesting to us that the Lord uses very similar language to Mosiah 29 when talking about the importance of partici-pation later in the Doctrine and Covenants: "Appoint among your-selves a teacher, and let not all be spokesmen at once; but let one speak at a time and let all listen unto his sayings, that when all have spoken that all may be edified of all, and that every man may have an equal privilege" (D&C 88:122).

Elder Richard G. Scott has taught, "Assure that there is abundant participation because that use of agency by a student authorizes the Holy Ghost to instruct. It also helps the student retain your message. As students verbalize truths, they are confirmed in their souls and strengthen their personal testimonies."[38] That's the same thinking behind the Church Educational System's invitation in its teaching emphasis to "help students learn how to explain, share, and testify of the doctrines and principles of the restored gospel. We are to give them opportunities to do so with each other in class." The CES hand-book for teaching, *Teaching the Gospel,* has long noted this principle:

> Learning has to be done by the pupil. Therefore it is
> the pupil who has to be put into action. When a

teacher takes the spotlight, becomes the star of the show, does all the talking, and otherwise takes over all of the activity, it is almost certain that he is interfering with the learning of the class members.[39]

The upshot of this collective counsel is clear: the more opportunities we give students to actively participate in the process of gaining insights (rather than sitting passively in class while we lecture), the more our students will retain those insights.

As former Harvard president Charles W. Eliot observed in his inaugural address nearly 150 years ago, "The lecturer pumps laboriously into sieves. The water may be wholesome, but it runs through. *A mind must work to grow.*"[40] In fact, research shows that twenty-four hours after a lesson, students recall only 5 percent of what they learn when taught primarily by lecture. Retention rises to 50 percent if students are taught primarily by discussion group, 70 percent when they practice by doing, and 90 percent when they teach each other and immediately put their learning to use.[41]

This kind of paradigm shift not only requires many of us to change our attitudes about the way we teach, but it requires us to help our students change their attitudes about the way they learn. As Elder Henry B. Eyring suggested to gospel students, "Rather than thinking, 'How good is [the teacher] going to be today?' you could think another way. You could say to yourself, 'What is it [the teacher] is trying to accomplish?' Then you could ask yourself quietly, 'What can I do to help?' . . . That choice of an attitude will change the way you listen."[42]

Okay, let's say I buy into the idea that my students and I need to make this change in our thinking. How do I get my students to make this change with me? What steps can I take to move the burden of learning from me as the teacher to my students?

King Mosiah's shift to a new form of government required a thorough explanation from the king—and some determined resistance to his people's repeated attempts to reflexively return to the old monarchical ways. We find it helpful to follow King Mosiah's example and spend some time at the beginning of each new semester or year helping students understand their obligation to learn by faith. For example, on the first day of class, Rob asks students to think about gospel classes in which they have learned more than in other classes. Since they are stuck with both him and the subject, he encourages them to focus on variables within their control. Virtually every semester, students themselves make the case quite persuasively for things like preparation, prayer, and participation. Eventually, most students respond much like King Mosiah's subjects, becoming "exceedingly anxious that every [student] should have an equal chance throughout all the [classroom]; yea, and every [student] expressed a willingness to answer for his [or her] own [learning]" (Mosiah 29:38).

Mark has observed that successful teachers also consistently train their students. As important as the first day is in laying the groundwork, if training stops there, most students will think the principles discussed that day are just another passing thing. In addition to giving students *opportunities* to share with each other in class, Mark notes, teachers who successfully have students take responsibility for their own learning provide *help* for their students to share with each other in class. These teachers will often prompt students with ideas such as, "Today, look for a footnote that you'd like to share with the class," or "Reread verses 1 through 15 and put a star by your favorite verse. Then be prepared to tell the rest of us why you liked it." This kind of continual training helps students become more confident and thus more likely to voluntarily participate in the class.

We also do everything we can to make sure students bring their own scriptures. If they don't, they're living on the spiritual dole. The next thing we do is try to get them to read on their own before the lesson.

That's kind of tough with a youth class on Sunday, where they're already reading something else for seminary.

Granted. But at least with seminary, institute, college religion, and adult Church classes, we try to be fairly adamant about our students reading before they come.

How do you do that?

At college and in seminary, we can and do make reading before class a major component of their grade.

That's cheating.

It's true; it's much easier in those settings to establish an expectation of reading. But even in those settings, we've found it important to send the message as the teacher that we expect our students to come prepared and that we're disappointed when they don't. Teachers can do a lot to reinforce the expectation of student preparation simply by reminding students what the next reading assignment is and by using language that implies their expectation that students are prepared (e.g., "What did you learn from the father's behavior in the parable of the prodigal son?"). It's not easy, but it is possible to create a culture where students feel that reading before class is almost as important as attending class itself. In Rob's law school experience, for example, that unwritten expectation was so firmly in place that students almost didn't dare come to class unprepared, even though reading wasn't part of their grade.

In observing teachers, Mark has also noticed that most teachers who report success in having seminary students read on their own have three things in place. First, they have a clear expectation that students will do the reading. Second, there is some kind of account-ability system, usually involving other students or the teacher knowing the status of the individual reader. Finally, they regularly give opportunities in class where students can talk with other class members about something that they have read. Rather than having a "devotional thought," the teacher invites students to orally share an insight from last night's scripture reading, or something along those lines. In classes where these three things are happening, over 80 percent of the students are reading on their own outside of class.

In summary, great gospel teachers make it clear that they expect their students to take responsibility for learning by faith.

Now that you mention it, I can remember some Gospel Doctrine classes where I felt like I really did have to do the reading before

class or I'd disappoint the teacher. I guess that made a difference to me. What else can teachers do to help students learn by faith?

They can model it.

What do you mean? Are you saying they should give an illustration of how to learn by faith?

Not formally. But when students see informal evidence that their teacher is also learning by faith, it shows them the way.

I'm still not sure I follow.

We love it when even some of the most knowledgeable teachers we know continue studying—and thus continue learning. That often comes through in the lesson. "Last night as I was reading this again, I noticed something I'd never noticed before." Such comments make it clear to students that the teacher is still paying the price to learn. Better yet, when students see a teacher highlight a new phrase in the scriptures or write a new note in the margin based on something a student said in class, students see that the teacher has come to class ready to learn—and willing to learn from students.

Rob still remembers attending a class at BYU where Professor Hugh Nibley talked about picking up a geometry textbook the night before and dabbling with some geometry. There was nothing boastful in Professor Nibley's comments, but his sheer love for learning was definitely inspiring.

You talked before about the importance of teaching students how to get insights instead of just giving them insights. Beyond expecting them to come prepared and showing them that you're still learning, how do you do that?

It's very helpful to remind students about some familiar tools as well as to show them new ones. This includes the marvelous and often underutilized study aids in the LDS scriptures, from footnotes to the Bible Dictionary. Beyond that, we like to show students the institute manuals that are available online at www.ldsces.org and how to use the search engine on www.lds.org.

We also try to demonstrate the techniques we use to glean insights rather than just sharing the insights. For example, we might invite students to take a look at the following excerpt from 2 Nephi 2:7–8:

> Behold, he offereth himself a sacrifice for sin, to answer the ends of the law, unto all those who have a broken heart and a contrite spirit; and unto none else can the ends of the law be answered.

> Wherefore, how great the importance to make these things known unto the inhabitants of the earth. . . .

We then note that we've circled the word *wherefore,* perhaps illustrating this visually on the chalkboard or a slide, and ask students what insights they get by focusing on that word.

> Behold, he offereth himself a sacrifice for sin, to answer the ends of the law, unto all those who have a broken heart and a contrite spirit; and unto none else can the ends of the law be answered.

> Wherefore, how great the importance to make these things known unto the inhabitants of the earth. . . .

Eventually, students realize that Lehi is teaching us that it's critical to share the gospel with our friends, because no one can meet the ends of the law without a broken heart and a contrite spirit and the Atonement of Jesus Christ. Before moving on from that particular insight, we point out that we can often find insights by remembering that words like *wherefore, for,* and *because* often connect the thought that precedes them with the thought that follows them. In the process, we've done more than just share an insight from 2 Nephi 2:7–8; we've shown students a tool they can use to find insights throughout the scriptures.

Finally, like our students, we often forget new skills if we don't have the chance to use them. So we give our students opportunities and excuses to use the tools we show them. We know some seminary teachers who feature a different study skill each week. They demonstrate the skill at the outset of the week and leave it written on a corner of the chalkboard as a reminder for students to try to use it throughout the week. More simply, teachers can assign tasks that call on these skills, such as, "Let me give you two minutes to find your favorite cross-reference to a verse on this page," or "Would someone check in the Bible Dictionary to see what the name *Abraham* means?" Or instead of directing students to a particular spot in the scriptures, we can ask them to find it themselves: "Let's turn to the story of David and Goliath," or "Can anyone find the passage in the Doctrine and Covenants that shows us that the Savior was tempted but never succumbed to the temptations?" After two or three students find the reference, we ask them to explain to the class how they found it.

In the college setting, Rob is able to give assignments that require students to use these skills. An incident involving one of these assignments demonstrates just what we are trying to accomplish with them. One Monday morning, Rob read an e-mail from a student with a doctrinal question. The next e-mail had been sent two hours later by the same student. She had just completed a quote portfolio assignment Rob had given his students that required them to search for General Authority quotes on www.lds.org. In the process, she had realized that she now had the ability to look up the answer to the question she had asked in her previous e-mail. She'd found the answer, she said, and no longer needed him to respond to the earlier e-mail!

It is precisely that kind of connection we hope students will make when we show them how to use tools and give them opportunities to use them.

These suggestions feel good but are still kind of basic. It seems like something more really needs to take place for students to learn by faith in the most meaningful way.

You're right. These kinds of tools really are just the building blocks. The final step we suggest is for teachers to make sure that they create plenty of opportunities for students to learn by faith in even more significant ways. Above all, teachers simply cannot afford to talk the whole time. This principle is so critical that we spend much of the next six chapters discussing various aspects of why and how to encourage students to participate. For now, let us just say that no matter how knowledgeable teachers are, they undermine students' opportunity and ability to learn by faith if they simply lecture in every lesson. "We primarily are to act and not only to be acted upon—especially as we seek to obtain and apply spiritual knowledge," explains Elder Bednar.[43] When we as teachers do all the acting, all too often our students merely end up being acted upon.

Beyond participating, our students need to learn by faith by cultivating a spirit of inquiry. Certainly one of the main reasons Joseph Smith received so many illuminating answers was that he asked so many good questions. Through instruction, example, and opportunity, we can teach our students to ask great questions. Before proceeding with his lesson, Rob recently started waiting until students ask at least one question about the scriptural text before he moves on with the lesson. More often than not, the first question triggers students to ask other questions that sometimes mushroom into an entire lesson. When students ask genuine, earnest, relevant questions, it's almost always a sure sign that learning by faith is occurring.

But in the one example of a student question you cited earlier in this chapter, Elder Bednar refused to answer the question. So what do you do with that? Are you allowed to answer questions?

Sometimes. But in the Spirit of allowing students to act rather than always acting on them, it's good to do a little triage. In the case of the question Elder Bednar was asked, he'd already given the student enough information to find the verse he was quoting. He knew that the student could find the verse simply by looking it up in the Topical Guide.

Other questions students ask may be great questions for a class discussion. If time permits, wise teachers often allow other students to try to answer the question first.

What if the other students don't know the right answer—or worse yet, they think they do, but they're wrong?

We'll discuss this more in the coming chapters, but gospel teachers always retain the responsibility for making sure correct doctrine is taught. So they might build on any truth they can find in a student's answer and then clarify or correct any errors as necessary.

Let us throw in one other possibility. When students ask a detailed doctrinal question that could be answered with a bit of research, an inspired teacher might direct students to a potential source or two rather than simply answering the question. Rob still remembers asking his teachers quorum adviser a question about the gathering and scattering of Israel. The adviser replied, "That's a great question, Rob. I want you to research it this week and let us know what you learn next week." Rob retained what he learned that week much better than he would have remembered any answer his teacher could have given him.

The teacher who can inspire students to learn out of class on their own truly helps them learn by faith. That leads to our last suggestion for creating learning opportunities for students: Whether with a formal assignment in college and seminary classes or an informal invitation to action in other classes, great learning often takes place when teachers or students plant ideas that inspire initiative—and then follow up on those suggestions.

Mark watched one teacher use a simple technique to inspire and then follow up on such out-of-class learning experiences. After the class had identified a gospel principle and the teacher had elicited comments about the application of the principle from the students, a student would share an experience of living the principle. Then the teacher elicited a concluding statement by asking a question such as, "So what have you learned from this?" After the student summarized the lesson learned, the teacher asked, "Do you have a challenge for the class?" Because the teacher had trained her students, they responded with an appropriate application "challenge" for their peers. The teacher had appointed a student to keep track of these challenges, and every couple of weeks the teacher asked the "tracker" to list off some of them. She then invited students to share any experiences and successes they had with taking a particular challenge.

Perhaps the highlight of each semester for Rob is reading students' papers summarizing their "Application Projects," in which they are asked to apply the doctrines they have been studying in some meaningful way outside of class. A few students just go through the motions to meet the minimum requirements for the project, but many others display great initiative and even have life-changing experiences as they apply gospel doctrines outside of class. Undoubtedly, students remember the insights gained from such individual efforts to learn by faith better than they remember any point Rob makes in class.

An experience of one of Mark's CES colleagues demonstrates this almost painfully. This brother was in his first year of teaching when a girl in his class handed him an envelope one day after class. After she left, he opened it and read a simple note that changed the way he taught forever. She wrote, "Tell me, and I'll forget. Show me, and I might remember. Involve me, and I'll understand."

It took courage for that girl to tell the teacher what he needed to hear. Her message hurt him at first, but he knew from that moment on that he needed to talk less and involve his students more if he was going to be an effective teacher.

- Remember that the best lessons are caught, not taught, and that great teachers help their students learn to catch the lessons.
- Help students understand what they can do to learn.
- Expect students to take responsibility for their learning.
- Show them that you're still learning by faith.
- Show them the tools they can use to glean insights for themselves—and give them a chance to use those tools.
- Cultivate a spirit of inquiry.
- Inspire and follow up on out-of-class learning and application.

FIVE

MAKE IT PERSONAL

President Boyd K. Packer has frequently stated that the "study of the doctrines of the gospel will improve behavior quicker than a study of behavior will improve behavior."[44] Unfortunately, a few gospel teachers use that quote as a basis for doing nothing more than teaching doctrine in the abstract, figuring the rest will take care of itself. They even seem to get annoyed with those who seek to help their students make the leap from understanding doctrine to applying it in their lives. "Apply the Resurrection," a colleague once challenged us, as if the Resurrection were a marvelous example of pure and powerful doctrine that couldn't be trivialized by applying it in some way to our daily lives. Others go beyond this and become so excited about newly discovered cultural, historical, geographic, political, or linguistic insights that they fail to teach the doctrine itself, let alone how to apply it in our lives.

Such teachers could improve their gospel lessons by asking the simple question President Packer himself likes to pose after hearing a presentation: "Therefore, what?"[45] Once, when Elder Oaks had a draft of one of his talks returned to him with that succinct response, the moral he drew from the story was that "the talk was incomplete because it omitted a vital element: what a listener should *do*."[46] So while great teachers teach doctrine, they also do so in a way that helps students connect doctrine with their lives. After all, as Elder Oaks has taught, great gospel teachers aim to have an "impact on the lives of the learners" and "will never be satisfied with just delivering a message or preaching a sermon."[47] The goal of great teachers is to help students apply doctrines and change their lives, not to help them win when playing Celestial Pursuit.

Fair enough. But if we focus so much on trying to get our students to change, isn't there some danger that we won't teach the doctrine? And by the way, how do you "apply" a doctrine like the Resurrection?

It's true that we can become so focused on standards that we fail to teach the doctrines underlying the standards. Helping students understand the doctrines and principles found in the scriptures is the critical first step. Once those are understood, students can apply the doctrines and principles in ways that will change their hearts, not just expand their minds. So as we strive to "liken all scriptures unto us, that it might be for our profit and learning" (1 Nephi 19:23), we must take care not to leave out the doctrine and jump straight to the application. We would never want to try to teach about the importance of modesty without first teaching the doctrinal basis for wearing modest clothes. On the other hand, it would be a shame to teach a doctrine like our bodies are temples without helping our students realize the ramifications of the doctrine.

Whether we're teaching about the Resurrection or the doctrine that our bodies are temples, we love to ask President Packer's probing question: "Therefore, what?" And yes, that works even for the Resurrection—especially for the Resurrection. When we ask students how knowledge of the Resurrection affects their lives, their comments usually fit into two groups. First, many will tell us what a difference the reality of the Resurrection has made for them when loved ones have died. Second, they tell us how differently they live their lives when they focus on the reality of an eternal afterlife. That's the kind of application Elder Oaks was talking about when he said,

> This hope changes the whole perspective of mortal life. The assurance of resurrection and immortality affects how we look on the physical challenges of mortality, how we live our mortal lives, and how we relate to those around us. . . . The assurance of resurrection also gives us a powerful incentive to keep the commandments of God during our mortal lives.[48]

So for us, and apparently for Elder Oaks, it's not a stretch at all to "apply" the Resurrection. It's a natural and important way to connect the doctrinal dots to our daily lives.

So if you were teaching a lesson about the Sabbath day, your goal would be to get students to do a better job of keeping the Sabbath?

Absolutely.

Doesn't that run contrary to this quote by Elder Oaks? "Teachers who are commanded to teach 'the principles of [the] gospel' and 'the doctrine of the kingdom' (D&C 88:77) should generally forgo teaching specific rules or applications. For example, they would not teach any rules for determining what is a full tithing, and they would not provide a list of dos and don'ts for keeping the Sabbath day holy. Once a teacher has taught the doctrine and the associated principles from the scriptures and the living prophets, such specific applications or rules are generally the responsibility of individuals and families."[49]

We know where you're coming from, and we've heard teachers use this quote before to justify their approach of simply teaching doctrine without attempting to facilitate application at all. It's important to understand Elder Oaks's comment in light of other comments that he and others have made. Remember, in that same talk Elder Oaks said that a gospel teacher should be "concerned with the results of his or her teaching." In fact, that's how teachers "will measure the success of [their] teaching and testifying"—"by its impact on the lives of the learners."[50] Elder Richard G. Scott echoed the importance of helping students apply doctrines and principles found in the scriptures to everyday living:

> Make your objective to help students understand, retain, and use divine truth. Keep that objective foremost in every aspect of your preparation and teaching. . . . The best measure of the effectiveness of what occurs in the classroom is to observe that the truths are being understood and applied in a student's life.[51]

Similarly, Church curriculum materials are clear in encouraging teachers to "help members understand, discuss, and apply [the prophets'] words. . . . Application questions will help participants see how they can live according to [the prophets'] teachings. For example, you might ask, 'What are some specific things we can do to share the gospel?'"[52]

I'm not quite sure I follow. How can all these things be true if "specific applications or rules are the responsibility of individuals and families"?

We think the best way to harmonize these statements is to view the teacher's role as *facilitating* rather than *dictating* application of doctrines and principles. When students themselves do the applying, we see at least three advantages. First, this avoids the situation where overzealous teachers, much like the Pharisees, push their own particular spin on a commandment. For example, we are on solid ground when we teach that "God's commandment for His children to multiply and replenish the earth remains in force."[53] We are on much shakier ground when we advocate specific interpretations of such doctrines (e.g., "This means couples should have as many children as they can provide for financially").

Second, even when we advocate a particular rule or application that is doctrinally sound, our timing may not be right.[54] By pushing specific applications prematurely, we may just be pushing some students away. Consider the Sabbath, one of the doctrines Elder Oaks singles out when cautioning against teaching specific rules or applications. As we contemplate our own journeys in living the law of the Sabbath more fully, we can see how our spiritual preparedness to accept certain principles has changed over time. Earlier in our lives, we might have been irritated rather than inspired by undue emphasis on the very same applications of the law of the Sabbath that we have since come to embrace and enjoy. If teachers insist on encouraging students to refrain from doing x on the Sabbath—even if that is something the Lord eventually wants them to refrain from doing—we may be interfering with our students' abilities to learn through the Spirit what the next step should be in *their* spiritual journeys. In many cases, that step will be more rudimentary than one we wish to emphasize; in some cases, it will be more advanced than anything we've tried personally.

The Lord seems to take our spiritual readiness into account when noting that He often inspires us with promptings rather than giving us additional commandments. In Doctrine and Covenants 63:22, the Lord promises to make His will known to us, but "not by the way of commandment, for there are many who observe not to keep my commandments." In other words, as we keep the commandments, He will give us more to work on, but often in the personal, customized promptings of the Spirit rather than in the broadcast form of a commandment. This helps those who are struggling to keep the commandments they've already received avoid greater condemnation.

Finally, when students liken doctrines to themselves rather than merely listening to teachers teach specific rules and applications, they are much more likely to remember and take to heart their inspired applications. As one of our students observed in response to a question about the benefits of participating in class, "I seem to remember those points the most that I verbalize in class." If this is true for gospel insights in general, it must be doubly true for doctrinal applications.

So how do I facilitate application rather than impose my own applications?

At the conclusion of every story or summary of doctrine, consider simply asking the students, "Therefore, what? What's the point? What's this got to do with the way I live? What should I focus on doing differently or striving to become, based on what we've read or discussed today?" Asking such questions at the end of every lesson is a good habit to create.[55]

Inviting students to look at a familiar story symbolically also opens their eyes to applications of doctrine. When teaching about Lehi's journey, we might ask students, "What did Lehi and his family have to leave behind to obtain a land of promise? What kinds of things do we have to leave behind as we seek to obtain personal lands of promise? What else can Lehi's journey teach us about our own journeys through life?" Our discussions of the war chapters in Alma come to life when we ask students what those chapters teach us about our own battles against evil.

Again, one of the greatest advantages to facilitating application by asking students questions is that it gives the Spirit the opportunity to teach them individually. Not only is the Spirit a much more effective teacher than we are, but the Spirit will always get the timing right in revealing to students what they need to know when they need to know it.

Mark has watched teachers invite students to personalize the applications that occur in a seminary class. For example, a student will often say something like, "When you follow the prophet's counsel to read the Book of Mormon, you're really doing what the Lord wants." Great teachers might follow up by asking, "Can you personalize that application? You said, 'you,' and I wonder if you could say that same thing but substitute the word *I* so that it becomes more personal to you." Then a bit haltingly, the student expresses the same principle in a much more personalized way: "Okay . . . when I read the Book of Mormon I know that I am following the prophet and doing what the Lord wants me to do." It's a simple change, but one that brings great power to the student and to the rest of the class.

One time a student in one of our classes accepted an invitation to pray and ask Heavenly Father for direction about what to work on next in life. She came to class the next day looking pretty frustrated. "I thought it would be easy," she fumed. "I thought that if I asked Heavenly Father for something to work on, He'd give me some little thing to work on. But no—He tells me I need to replace my entire wardrobe. I like my wardrobe, and I think it's just fine. But apparently Heavenly Father thinks it's too immodest, and now I've got to replace the whole thing."

There had been no mention of immodesty in the previous lesson, let alone any suggestion that this particular student's blouses were too revealing. But when she took on the job of applying the doctrines we'd discussed in class, she'd received a very clear and very challenging prompting. And because the Spirit had given the application directly to her, she couldn't argue with her teacher about necklines. At the beginning of the next class, she brought in a stack of pink hangers and threw them on the floor in mock disgust. As she later explained to the class, she actually felt great for acting on a customized prompting from the Spirit. By assuming the burden of learning, this student had allowed the Spirit to teach her in a way that no other instructor ever could.

- Teach with the real purpose in mind.
- Help students understand the doctrines and principles.
- Then help them connect the doctrinal dots by applying doctrines to their lives.
- Facilitate rather than dictate application.

SIX

LOOK WHO'S TALKING

For both of us, the single most important thing we've learned about improving our gospel teaching in the past decade would be doing more to draw the students into the lesson and the process of learning. We both believed this was important before and did it to some extent, but in the last decade we have come to believe it's even more important than we originally thought. We've learned that participation—and lots of it—is simply an essential ingredient in a great lesson. We've also learned some things about how to get students to participate meaningfully.

And it's not just us. Whether it's becoming convinced that student participation really is essential to great gospel teaching, or whether it's learning how to generate more student participation, we see more room for improvement in this aspect of gospel teaching than in any other area. That's why we end up recommending this chapter and the ones that follow it more than any others to friends who ask for advice.

So general conference talks aren't great lessons?

Well, not exactly. They're great talks, but they're not great lessons because they're not really lessons.

There's a time and a season for everything. Mark enjoys speaking at Especially For Youth, where it's much more difficult to have interactive teaching and individual participation because of the size of the groups he's speaking to. The same is definitely true of general conference and even sacrament meeting talks. But whether we're teaching

Gospel Doctrine or Primary or anything in between, it's important to remember that lessons are different from talks and that student participation is a key ingredient to a great lesson.

But why? I have to admit, I'm much more comfortable lecturing. Shouldn't I just play to my strengths rather than try to be some kind of teacher I'm not?

Some teachers may naturally be more disorganized or more boring or less prepared. But that's not much of a reason for refusing to improve. And when it comes to gospel teaching, we have to agree with the pointed advice Elder Richard G. Scott gave a group of CES teachers: "Never, and I mean never, give a lecture where there is no student participation. A 'talking head' is the weakest form of class instruction."[56]

Why is having student participation so much better?

For starters, we've found that our students learn more when they're awake and paying attention. And they're more likely to stay awake and focused when more people participate—and especially when they participate themselves.

Second, when teachers lecture, the data bank of insights and experience available to the Spirit is quite limited. When we open the classroom to our students, that data bank suddenly increases dramatically because each student's experiences, insights, and testimony are now in play. For example, while discussing the story of Nephi's broken bow last year, we invited our students to share some insight they had about the story. One amateur archer in the class noted that Nephi fashioned not only a new bow, but a new arrow—even though the text mentions only his bow being broken (see 1 Nephi 16:18–23). The student explained that different types of bows require different types of arrows. Because Nephi made his new bow from wood rather than steel, this student observed, it made perfect sense that he would also have to fashion a new arrow.

Did we know more about the Book of Mormon generally than this student did? Hopefully. But we had never noticed this authenticating detail before. Our student's insight was just one of many things we have learned from the impressive pool of our students' collective knowledge. Much of that knowledge comes from our students' experience: being an avid archer, having divorced parents, being a racial minority, having to choose between being in a successful rock band and serving a mission, living in Saudi Arabia as an American citizen, having joined the Church despite the objections of parents, and having raised sheep, to name just a few of the many experiences our students have brought to discussions that we could not. While serving as president of BYU—Idaho, Elder David A. Bednar recognized how much teachers can learn from their students. On a number of occasions he said that "any faculty member at BYU—Idaho who does not believe that he or she can learn something from a student does not deserve to be a faculty member at BYU—Idaho."[57]

Third, when we're talking about teaching children, youth, or even young adults, students' comments tend to carry more weight with other students than teachers' comments do. There's something uniquely powerful about a student's peers testifying about a principle that makes it even more convincing than hearing it from the teacher. When Rob served as a bishop, his ward had a missionary preparation campout for its young men, and he invited some recently returned missionaries. They told stories, answered questions, role-played, and bore testimonies around the campfire. The next morning when Rob asked one of the priests how he'd enjoyed it, he said it was pretty good—especially the recently returned missionaries: "It's not like it's been twenty years since they went on their missions." That stung a bit, since it *had* been twenty years since Rob had gone on his mission. Even though those young men could still learn plenty from Rob's experience, they were a lot more willing to listen to people closer to their own age.

Part of this is a perception problem, but part of it's legitimate: when a teenager in class testifies about the blessings that come from standing up to friends who want to watch bad videos, the fact is that the young person's testimony carries a lot of weight because the students know their friend lives in their world. We resist watching bad videos, but as married guys settled down in life, our experience is completely different. So whether it's just perception or there are legitimate grounds for it, we know that many of the most convincing comments and testimonies that will be made in our classes will come from students, not us.

One of Mark's recent projects in the training division of CES was to gather student testimonials of this kind of teaching and make them into a video. Here are two of the many examples he's collected of how students feel about the comments they hear from other students:

- "We may be in some ways on the same level. We're all from different backgrounds, we've all gone through different things, and so we all have different experiences that we can draw from and share with the class. And we all have different comments with a different Spirit that can be shared."

- "Sometimes when [other students] share their feelings they mention struggles that they've had or times when they've doubted the gospel and how they found out that it was true. And you go, 'I'm not the only one in this world that has ever doubted, and so I won't be the only one who's ever received an answer.'"

Okay, I can see that there could be some situations where comments from students could be quite helpful, maybe even better than a lecture from the teacher. But when I'm teaching them about doctrines they may not already understand, not just asking them about their feelings or experiences, don't I pretty much have to be the teacher at that point?

It's true that some points in your lesson will lend themselves to participation better than others. We'll talk about this more in the next few chapters as we discuss how to get students to participate in the lesson. But getting students to participate in the learning process is more than just another way to create some diversity in your lesson. It's a better approach to getting students to learn. We'll add that to the list as the fourth reason, but it may be the most important one of all.

What's the fourth reason?

Students learn better when they participate in teaching truths. As students teach each other, they will be taught more perfectly; as more students have the privilege to participate, more students will be edified. Just like we remember our way to a destination better when we are driving than when we're just along for the ride, students remember insights much better when they have to come up with them rather than just copying them down. When we teach each other diligently, we're promised that the Lord's grace will attend us—not that we may instruct more perfectly, but that we "may *be instructed* more perfectly in theory, in principle, in doctrine, in the law of the gospel, in all things that pertain unto the kingdom of God" (D&C 88:78; emphasis added). As we teach or participate, we learn—and we learn more perfectly.

Let's say that on the first day of a Sunday School class or a new semester in seminary, you wanted to convince students about some of the benefits of participation that we've just discussed. Many of them, probably most of them, have never considered the issue before. So you could just tell them: here are three reasons our class will be better if you participate. But that kind of passive learning is much less memorable than if the students are challenged to come up with the same insights themselves, aided by leading or thought-provoking questions. A teacher might ask students, "Why do you get more out of classes where you participate?" In the very process of coming up with answers to that question, students gain insights they are more likely to remember. And as a teacher, by facilitating it you just illustrated the very thing that you are emphasizing: the value of student participation.

That's the Socratic method at its best—teaching students through a series of questions that lead them to draw certain conclusions for themselves. It may take a little longer than just telling students what you want them to know, but it's much more effective.

Okay, maybe this works when you get to the part of the lesson where you want students to discuss their feelings about the doctrines. But if I don't lecture on the doctrines themselves, how will the students learn?

All of Rob's professors at Stanford Law School were both more intelligent and more knowledgeable than he was, yet they almost universally taught by asking questions rather than by lecturing. With probing questions, his professors gave their students opportunities to articulate principles they had just learned by reading—and to gain other insights they had not yet even considered. Similarly, President Kim Clark once experienced "something truly remarkable" during a class discussion while he was the dean of the Harvard Business School. "My role was like that of an orchestra conductor," he explained, "as [my students] made comments, challenged each other, debated each other, taught each other, clarified, added to, and kept taking us deeper." As he facilitated the discussion among his students rather than simply lecturing to them, both President Clark and his students participated in "an extraordinary learning experience."[58]

Maybe this works in graduate schools with motivated students, but I'm thinking of a Sunday School class of carpet-watching teenagers—guys who just sit there in the deacon position: slouched over, elbows on their knees, heads down as if they're studying the carpet. It's hard to imagine them participating much, let alone deducing eternal truths.

Sometimes it's a matter of training, tradition, and expectation. If they've been in classes where teachers weren't really committed to getting them to participate, they figure they can just float along while teachers spoon out gospel truths. There's no doubt that change requires real effort.

Sustained effort, too. Remember how we talked about Tiger Woods having the courage to overhaul his swing? Well, what was especially impressive about his making that change was that the improvement didn't come quickly. In fact, he got a little worse before he got better. Your classes won't get any worse if you try to get students involved. But it may take a while for you—and for your students—to adapt to this approach if they're not used to it. Most students know that if a new teacher does try to instigate some participation, they can get him or her to go back to lecturing if they stick together in silence for a few seconds after those first questions are asked. Uncomfortable with the awkwardness, most teachers throw in the towel and go back to lecturing. But if you stay the course, you can get students of almost any age to participate regularly.

The bottom line is that teachers shouldn't give up if students don't respond immediately when they try to get them to participate more actively in learning. Nor should teachers be satisfied simply because they've had a wonderful lesson where students felt the Spirit. Students must learn how to invite the Spirit into their own scripture study to become more spiritually independent. After four years of reading scriptures and asking students, "What can we learn from this for our own lives?" a seminary teacher's hope is that students can and will do that for themselves—on their own. Youth leaders, seminary teachers, and parents won't always be there to dole out gospel truths. Encouraging active student participation—especially in applying the scriptures to our lives—cultivates students' ability to learn.

This sounds good, but I often struggle to get through all the material when I do all the talking. I fear that I'll have to sacrifice substance for content if I open my class up to participation. Every minute of discussion takes away another minute I needed to cover the material.

That would be true—if the only effective teaching occurred while teachers were lecturing. But rather than merely tread water, great classroom discussions actually cover ground. Guided by capable teachers, in fact, discussions cover much or most of the ground teachers otherwise would have covered themselves.

Even if you don't cover quite as much material with discussion as you do while lecturing, the goal is not simply to cover material. Elder Scott reminds us: "Remember, your highest priority is not to get through all the material if that means that it cannot be properly absorbed. Do what you are able to do with understanding. . . . Determine . . . what is of highest priority."[59] We'd much rather cover 80 percent of the material and have our students awake and engaged than cover 100 percent of the material and have our students asleep.

What if I open up my class for discussion and students say things that are off base? It feels like I'm giving up doctrinal control when I allow discussion.

Great teachers never relinquish control of the classroom. They may choose to allow a discussion to wind down a different path than they had originally planned, but they are still ultimately responsible for navigating. That means that even as they hear insights that are new to them, they're responsible for sifting through ideas to make sure that any dross is purged from the gold. Just as bishops remain responsible for the doctrinal content of sacrament meetings, teachers who invite participation in classrooms can and should make sure that students aren't left with any doctrinal confusion.

I've got a friend who's a great Gospel Doctrine teacher, and he says all this talk about student participation just amounts to gimmicks. He says that when we emphasize the style of teaching so much, we slight the substance, and that great style can never compensate for bad content. The main thing is that he teaches truth, he says; the rest is just so much frosting on the cake.

There's no question that we'd all be better off teaching true doctrines poorly than teaching false doctrines well. And it's important that we not lose sight of gaining expertise and sound understanding of what we teach, even as we focus on how to teach well. But we are sorely mistaken if we think we succeed as long as we teach truth, regardless of how bad our techniques may be. In fact, the Lord's famous query about whether we are teaching the "word of truth . . . by the Spirit of truth or some other way" (D&C 50:17) squarely contradicts the notion that it's enough just to teach truth. Even if we're teaching the truth, if we do not teach it by the Spirit, "it is not of God" (D&C 50:18).[60]

We're not suggesting that student participation is the Lord's way, while lecturing is not of God. Teacher presentation certainly has a place in the classroom. But this passage does remind us that teaching truth alone doesn't guarantee that our teaching will be effective. If our students are to learn truth, we have to be concerned about not only what we teach, but also the way we teach it. Granted, it's possible to become so obsessed with methodology that we lose sight of substance. But if we criticize every discussion of teaching methodology as merely being "gimmicks," we've effectively excused ourselves from any need to scrutinize the way we teach and from trying to improve.

SEVEN
OPENERS

It's one thing to believe that students ought to participate in class and quite another to be able to get them to. In this chapter we move beyond making a case for participation to discussing how to make it happen. And perhaps nothing does more to draw students out of themselves and into the lesson than a great use of the first few minutes of class. We call that beginning our Opener. Ask Mark if he's ready to teach the next day's lesson, and no matter how well prepared the rest of his lesson his, he will tell you he's not ready until he's got a good Opener.

What makes the beginning of class so important?

Think about the best and worst starts you ever had to a date as a teenager. Those beginnings alone didn't guarantee a good or bad date, but it was sure hard to recover from showing up and asking for your date by the wrong name. On the other hand, if you and your buddies managed to get a limousine for your prom dates, you went a long way to having a great evening together. Just like how you begin a date, how you begin a lesson matters *a lot*.

Let's say your subject is section 4 of the Doctrine and Covenants. You could begin by simply having students open up to section 4 and then talking about it, but you risk losing all but the most diligent students.

So I should have them open up *Sports Illustrated* instead? Or maybe I should tap dance?

No, neither of us can tap dance. And if we could, we still wouldn't. We're not there to entertain these students—we're there to teach them the gospel. But it is important to start lessons in a way that will draw students *into the lesson* and *out of themselves.* We call our technique Openers, because these methods not only open the lesson, but if you do them right, they open up the students too.

This may not sound like much, but it's probably the single most important thing Rob learned from watching Mark as he made his transition into CES. Mark spends about 30 percent of his preparation time coming up with the first five minutes of his lesson. As Rob has tried to incorporate the things Mark does in his Openers, he's been amazed at what a difference it makes for his entire lesson—especially the level of class participation.

So what do you do—start with an object lesson to get their attention?

It's more than that, really. We've got three objectives in mind for our Opener, and an object lesson alone won't necessarily accomplish all three. First, we want to grab students' attention. We need something interesting to get the ball rolling. Second, we want to help them make the transition from their everyday world into a gospel discussion. We want to ease them into class, not throw them in the deep end.

You could do both of those things with an object lesson.

You could, but an object lesson alone doesn't accomplish our third and perhaps most important purpose, which is to stimulate participation. We want to get as many students as we can to feel safe talking at the beginning of class so they'll feel comfortable participating later. Let us illustrate with a dry, counterproductive approach first: "All right, class, open your books to Doctrine and Covenants section 4. This section is about missionary work. Many of you boys will be missionaries, right? So according to section 4, what are the qualities that a good missionary needs? Anyone . . . anyone?"

Is that really such a bad question, as long as you don't sound like a dry teacher?

No, not really. But even with a good question, jumping straight into a gospel discussion can be difficult for kids who are just waking up or even for adults who are just settling into class. We aim for something that is both more subtle and more exciting.

Like what?

For section 4, how about this? Give everyone in the class a page from the classified ads and 60 seconds to find two jobs—one they most wish they could have and one for which they're the most qualified right now. When they're done, have several students share what they've come up with.

That sounds interesting but pretty time consuming for something that's not particularly relevant.

It's not especially relevant yet, but that's the beauty of it. Students, especially youth, are much more apt to start talking about something like this than they are to answer a gospel question right off.

But what if they get going on whatever bizarre jobs they've come up with?

We hope they do. That's one of the main objectives of our Openers—to lower the entrance barriers to participation, to make it easy for students to participate by giving them something to discuss that's interesting to them. We like to ask questions or provide topics where they can't go wrong.

But there's only so much time. How can you afford to spend time letting students just talk about things that don't directly relate to the lesson?

Eventually they do relate, but we understand your concern. The first few times Rob watched Mark teach, he thought the same thing. Rob kept looking at the time and wondering how he was going to cover all the material. Yet somehow, the rest of his lesson didn't seem rushed at all. And he had the students' attention and participation from the outset.

Consider it an investment. You have to be careful not to get carried away, but spending a few minutes at the outset of class to set things up well makes the remainder of the lesson much more productive. One day one of us was unprepared with an Opener and started by doing exactly what we're telling you not to do—just having students open up their scriptures. One girl in the front row actually blurted out, "You can't do that. You can't just jump into the scriptures. I'm not ready yet." We were embarrassed for our lack of preparation that day but were pleased that the Openers we'd been using the rest of the year had apparently been working.

And it's not just wasted time on some irrelevant subject, either. With this Opener, for example, once they've had a chance to loosen up and talk about the jobs they chose, we discuss how the most rewarding jobs can require years of experience and training. We then ask them to spend 60 seconds creating a list of qualifications for the job of being a full-time missionary. When they're done, they share their answers quite freely because they're warmed up. Then we plunge into section 4 to see what the Lord set forth as the qualifications for serving Him.

Okay, I have to admit that's better than just having students turn to a chapter of scripture. But what if I'm not creative?

We suspect you're more creative than you realize. And the more you work at it, the more creative you can become.

When I look at the classified ads, I see a lot of boring small print, not a potential idea for a lesson. I couldn't come up with an Opener like that off the top of my head.

We didn't. We actually came up with the Opener the night before our lesson when we were looking at the newspaper. And earlier in the day we'd spent fifteen or twenty minutes trying to come up with the right Opener for that lesson. It will probably be harder for you, at least at first. But you really can develop the ability to come up with these things. We know teachers who claimed to have no creativity but kept working at it, and eventually they have been able to come up with some pretty good Openers.

How?

First, always look for one in the manual. Sometimes the manual has a great one, and you can use it exactly as directed. Sometimes it will spark an idea in your mind, and you can use some variation of it. Second, borrow freely from other teachers' good ideas.

Isn't that plagiarism?

Only if you claim you made it up when you didn't. We give other people credit whenever we can, or we'll ask them if we can use their idea. But teaching the gospel isn't a competition, so most people are happy if others use their good ideas.

Realistically, when am I going to see other teachers in action?

Probably not nearly as much as you'd like. But you can pick up a lot of ideas at in-service or teacher training meetings. And there will always be others in your ward and stake teaching the same lessons. Connect with a couple of them and share ideas every week. That can be invaluable.

Another thought is to look for Openers in advance. It's true that it can be difficult if you have to come up with them on the spot. So we like to scan the next twenty lessons and even spend some time in the summer or between semesters trying to come up with better Openers. We keep them in the back of our minds so that when we're looking at the classified ads, we remember that section 4 has the Lord's qualifications for missionaries, and we make the connection. Sometimes we'll even jot the idea down on a Post-it and stick it in the manual next to an upcoming lesson.

You can even look for object lessons that would make great Openers without knowing yet what principle you'd use them to illustrate. We're always looking for cool science experiments and then seeing what gospel principle they might be tied to.

But those are basically object lessons. I thought you guys were above that.

Not at all. We love object lessons. We just want to emphasize that a starter needs an additional element that object lessons don't necessarily have: student participation. We could do a marvelous object lesson and explain what it means, and it would help grab students' attention and draw them into the lesson. But if they haven't talked, it hasn't drawn them out of themselves. So rather than having the teacher draw the conclusions from the object lesson, we have the students draw them.

One of Mark's favorites, which is not exactly an object lesson, is comparing a scar to repentance. Scars never really go away, but sins do through repentance.

But scars are evidence of a healing process.

So Mark asks his students to tell him how scars are similar to or different from repentance.

But that seems like kind of a deep question to start with.

It is. That's why we don't start with that question. Instead we ask how many students have a scar, and then we let a few of them share the stories behind their scars. It's amazing how many students have stories and how eager they are to share their stories. And you're right—if we'd started with the comparison between sin and scars, not as many students would have volunteered an answer. That's what we're talking about when we say that a good starter lowers the bar for participation, and it's the key to great Openers. We take the time to ask questions students are comfortable answering, questions that don't have wrong answers and don't require any real gospel knowledge.

At the law school Rob attended, professors usually just randomly called on students to participate, which kept students on their toes. But one of his professors actually forewarned three students at a time that they would be on the hot seat on a particular day. Rob uses this in his classes at BYU—Idaho, and he calls it the Friendly Hot Seat. The law professor didn't exactly lower the bar like we've been describing, but for law school, just letting students know that they were going to be grilled on a particular day was lowering the bar. It let students prepare, and the professor made sure they had a good experience.

And the difference it made in class was amazing. In other classes, 20 to 50 percent of the students would volunteer comments. In this professor's class, by the end of the semester, after everyone had taken their turn on the panel, 50 to 80 percent of the students were volunteering comments. You could see a direct correlation between whether students had had their turn in the Friendly Hot Seat and whether they were willing to participate in class. The professor was creating a safe opportunity for them to participate, to hear their voice in class without embarrassing themselves. That helped them overcome a mental barrier to joining in the discussion and really opened the floodgates to broad participation in her classes.

So you lower the bar by asking them about scars?

Or a time they've forgotten something when they went on trip (think 1 Nephi 3) or a time someone broke a promise to them (great for a lesson on covenants) or what the hardest thing is about going to a new school. Think about the young man in your class who will be least likely to participate. Now try to imagine him answering a question cold about listing the qualities the Lord wants in His missionaries. If he does have an answer in mind, he's probably not very confident that it's a good answer. And the last thing he wants to do is give the wrong answer to a question or look stupid. Some students are even embarrassed to give answers they know are right, because they don't want to look like know-it-alls.

So we try to begin by asking interesting questions that don't really have wrong answers. That young man in your ward is a lot more likely to tell you the story about the scar he got skateboarding than he is to answer a question about important traits for missionaries.

Maybe I should just give a whole lesson on skateboarding.

We're not saying that, not at all. And you're right in suggesting that we've got to be careful about how much time to spend on an Opener.

We cringe when we hear about teachers who never get around to getting students into the scriptures. Even with an Opener, our students are usually in the scriptures within five minutes of the prayer at the longest. And frankly, when we're teaching adults or students who are quite willing to participate, we don't lower the bar quite as much or take as much time drawing them in. Over the course of the semester, we can often move to the core of the lesson more quickly as rapport from previous lessons carries over.

But we are saying that your typical reluctant young man or shy young woman is a lot more likely to answer a gospel question if you start out with a much less threatening topic of discussion. It's likening the scriptures unto us, but in reverse order. We start by talking about everyday things the kids can relate to, and then we jump back to the scriptures—all of which allows us to liken the scriptures to ourselves.

In the end, for our lesson about section 4, we want kids to realize that just as it takes years of preparation to qualify for really cool jobs, it takes years of preparation to qualify to truly serve the Lord as a missionary. And He's told us exactly what qualifications are required for the job. A good Opener not only grabs their attention, eases them into the lesson, and prepares them to participate, but it also sets the theme for a lesson that ultimately applies the scriptures to their lives in a way they can remember.

Great Openers

Grab students' attention.

Ease students into a gospel discussion.

Stimulate participation.

- Consider time spent on the Opener as an investment.
- Look in the manual for Opener ideas.
- Borrow ideas from other teachers.
- Look for Openers in advance.
- Use Openers to get students into the scriptures, not to replace the scriptures.

EIGHT

THE ART OF CRAFTING QUESTIONS

Great questions are the backbone of great lessons. That's why crafting great questions should be viewed as an art, not an afterthought. In fact, once we've become familiar with the material we're teaching, we probably spend more time coming up with good questions than we do working on any other aspect of preparing a lesson. In this chapter, we explore some basic principles and rules for crafting useful questions.

I can never come up with great questions on the fly.

Fortunately, you don't really have to.

Why not?

Because you can and should come up with most of your questions in advance. The first principle of formulating great questions is that you should really invest some time in coming up with them. Don't just assume they'll take care of themselves during the lesson itself.

When we prepare our lessons, we like to spend some time brainstorming about different questions we could ask. As teachers master the craft of asking great questions, they can come up with some pretty good lessons on the spot. But the bottom line is that your lessons will be better if you invest some real mental energy in coming up with questions that will spark discussion and involve students in learning for themselves.

So when you're crafting your questions, what do you aim for? How do you know when you've got a good question?

Here's the measuring stick we use in judging a question: would we be willing or tempted to answer the question ourselves if we were students in the class? If not, we figure others probably won't respond to it either.

Note that there are two extremes to avoid: questions that are too easy and questions that are too difficult.

Too easy? Why is that a problem? Isn't that just part of lowering barriers to entry?

Sometimes teachers end up asking questions to which the answers are so obvious (e.g., "How often should we read the scriptures?") that there's just no point in answering them, so no one does. Ironically, if everyone knows the answer to a straightforward question already, it's often hard to get anyone to answer.

So you should just ask questions that only the smart kids can answer?

No, but you should ask questions that require at least some thought or effort. Every once in a while when our questions draw a blank, we realize that we've asked a question that's so obvious, no one sees any real point in answering it. On the other hand, questions that are too difficult—especially questions with only one right answer— are just as deadly.

What do you mean, "just one right answer"? Don't most questions have just one real right answer?

It's true that some questions have only one right answer, and occasionally you may want to ask some of those questions. But tough, factual questions are a high-risk proposition that scare most kids away. If we ask students who appeared on the Mount of Transfiguration with Christ and Moses, some won't have any clue; some will know enough to be confused about whether it was Elias, Elijah, or John the Baptist; and the one kid who knows may not want to answer the question because he or she will look like a show-off. So no one answers the question.

Generally speaking, factual questions aren't particularly thought provoking, although they can be useful if you're directing students to search for something in a particular passage of scripture. Closed-ended questions in general—questions with a *yes* or *no* answer or a simple factual answer—rarely lead to much discussion. Contrast those kinds of questions with questions that have multiple good answers, such as, "Why is forgiving other people so important? Why do we have to forgive people, even if they don't repent or say they're sorry? How do you feel when you harbor grudges against other people?" Those are the kinds of questions we want—what Elder Scott refers to as "carefully formulated questions that stimulate thought" and "motivate discussion."[61]

We've discovered that there's great power in using the same principles in conducting interviews as a bishop or a father. Questions like, "Are you living like you should?" don't usually trigger much of a discussion. We have much more success with questions like, "Tell me which of the standards in *For the Strength of Youth* is most challenging for you." Or, "Think about a time in your life when you felt closest to the Lord. How does that compare to right now? What things were you doing differently then?" Or for a youth or adult who's drifting, this kind of question may help him or her open up: "Paint three pictures for me of what life could be like for you five years from now—a realistic worst-case scenario, a realistic best-case scenario, and where you think you're actually headed."

But I like straightforward questions with clear answers. Are you saying I can't ever ask closed-ended questions?

No, of course not. A closed-ended question has its place. Different kinds of questions work best for different situations or purposes. Let's say you're teaching a lesson about the children of Israel murmuring. One of the basic factual points you might want to make is that the Israelites murmured again just three days after the parting of the Red Sea. That basically calls for a closed-ended question with one right answer.

So why don't you just tell them?

Sometimes we do, but it's a lot easier for students to miss the significance of a fact like that if we just tell them than if they have to find it themselves.

I thought you weren't supposed to ask obscure factual questions?

Generally, we don't. But when we're pointing students to a particular passage of scripture and asking them to draw something out of it, it can be a productive reading exercise. And those kinds of questions often help lay the groundwork for stimulating and meaningful questions by getting students into the material or a particular subject.

The art of asking good questions in a class is a lot like the art of making good conversation. We often need to lead up to the most interesting questions with more simple factual questions. So before we get to application questions, we might first want to ask some basic questions that help our students focus on certain phrases or facts in a passage of scripture. We might ask, "Just where did Lot pitch his tent?" We could then follow up those kinds of questions with more probing analytical questions: "What's the problem with pitching your tent *toward* Gomorrah as long as you're not actually camping *in* Gomorrah?" Then students are better prepared to apply the principles from the story to their lives. "How are we sometimes tempted to pitch our tents, figuratively speaking, toward Gomorrah?"

The beauty of application questions is that there are usually a number of different useful ways to answer, which means that lots of people can answer the same question. Once someone answers your closed-ended, factual question correctly, there's not a lot more you can do with it. But you can spend a whole period listening to different students give different, helpful answers to questions like how we can be more in tune with the Lord so that we'll receive more inspiration in our lives.

And the fact that there are so many possible good answers makes those questions less threatening to students. Like good Openers, application questions tend to lower barriers of entry to discussion, making it easier for people to participate. And in classes where you have a broad range of levels of gospel knowledge and experience, application questions are marvelously elastic.

What do you mean by "elastic"?

Ask a question like, "So what are some things we can do to make sure we're really communicating with God and not just going through the motions when we pray?" and you can get great answers from a new convert or a returned mission president. You don't need to have read Hugh Nibley to answer questions like that. And even if you are a great gospel scholar, you can probably learn something useful from listening to the answer of even the newest member. With factual questions, on the other hand, you can't add anything to the discussion if you don't know the answer already—and if you do know the answer already, you won't gain much from the discussion.

Finally, we need to add one last point here about crafting great questions: No fishing.

Fishing?

That's when teachers ask a difficult question with a particular answer in mind and then won't accept any answer but the one they have in mind. Here's a classic bad example of what we're talking about. Once in a Gospel Doctrine class we heard someone answer a question by saying something like, "I was reading in the Bible Dictionary last week, and it pointed out something I hadn't noticed before on this point." Then he read a few sentences from the Bible Dictionary. To us, it seemed like a pretty good answer. But apparently this wasn't the exact answer the teacher was fishing for, so he said, "No, that's not it. Anybody else?"

Of course, nobody else really wanted to risk answering at that point. That's one of the worst things about fishing. Pretty soon the class realizes that the only acceptable answers are the ones the teacher already has in mind, and they get tired of trying to read the teacher's mind. So they stop participating.

Fishing may not be so bad if you're asking a factual question that really has only one factual answer, especially if you're pointing students to a particular passage of scripture where they can find the answer. But we often see teachers fishing with questions that don't necessarily have just one right answer, like, "What's the single most important thing you can do to prepare for a mission?" There are several good answers you could give—repent, live worthily, share the gospel, study the scriptures. Frankly, when teachers fish for answers, the one answer they have in mind may not even be the best answer, which just aggravates students all the more.

There's no need for that, and there's an easy way around it. Let's say you want to make a point about the importance of sharing the gospel with your own friends before going on a mission, and you think it's the single most important thing someone can do to prepare for a mission. Maybe it is, maybe it isn't. Instead of asking what the single most important thing someone can do to prepare for a mission is—and rejecting all answers other than sharing the gospel with your friends—ask what some of the things are that prospective missionaries could do to help prepare themselves for a mission—and accept all answers with merit. That question gives someone the opportunity to make the particular point you have in mind, and it also opens the door to a lot of other useful insights, including some you don't have in mind.

In fact, almost anytime we have a list of points we're hoping to make—like seven ways to improve prayer or four critical things to prepare for a mission—we try to ask a question that will allow students to make as many of those points as possible. Your motto could be, "Ask before you list." When you see a list of points in your lesson, make sure you put a question before it.

But what if they don't come up with the points you're thinking of?

No problem. After listening to all of theirs, you can always throw in a couple of points yourself. Their lists will rarely match yours completely, but some of the best points may be things you didn't even have on your list.

How about the other extreme? What if they come up with all your points? Then you've got no lesson left.

That's one way to look at it. We'd look at it as a moral victory. The more information and insights we can get the students to articulate themselves, the more they will remember. In fact, that might be a good final step in crafting questions for a lesson. Look at your lesson plan and ask yourself, "What questions could I add that would allow students to make more of the points I'm hoping to make?"

- Invest time in creating questions.
- Ask questions you would want to answer.
- Use questions with multiple "right answers"—they work especially well.
- Remember that different types of questions work best for different purposes.
- Avoid fishing!
- Ask before you list.

NINE

THE ART OF ASKING QUESTIONS

We've seen plenty of teachers read perfectly good questions from the manual without getting much of a response. There's an awkward silence for a second or two, and then the teacher quickly moves on with the lesson and gives up on having a discussion. Crafting good questions is an art, but so is asking them. In this chapter we explore the art of asking questions well.

You can't just read the questions?

Asking questions well really begins before class even starts.

Didn't we cover that in the last chapter on the art of crafting questions?

That's important, too, but we're talking about getting some banter going with students before class. Here's the basic idea: it's hard for anyone to be the first one to break the ice. And the thicker the ice is, the harder it is to break. Sometimes teachers haven't talked with students at all before class, and they haven't begun their lesson with a good Opener. So when they finally ask a question, it seems almost abrupt. Everything since the opening prayer has been the teacher talking, and now suddenly some brave soul has to be the first one to answer a question. That's tough for teenagers or younger kids; it's even pretty hard for adults.

So you're saying that by asking students how their basketball game went—or whatever else it is you ask teenagers about—you lower the barriers to entry?

Exactly. Even with a prayer and song in between, when you've established rapport with the students before class, it's almost as if the conversation lingers in the air, and it's easier to resume a conversation once class starts than if you're coming in cold. That's especially true if you pick up the flow with a good Opener. Between pre-class chatter and a good Opener, the basic idea is to start early in creating a conversational climate. By getting discussions going before class and at the outset of class on comfortable topics, you've established the classroom as a place where discussions occur. This can be as simple as greeting adults and visiting with them as they come into a Gospel Doctrine class or playfully teasing some of the kids in a Primary setting.

That leads us to an important related idea: make the classroom safe. It's imperative for teachers to make sure students don't feel attacked or belittled in the classroom, by other students or especially by the teacher. Virginia H. Pearce said it best:

> Learning occurs best in an atmosphere of trust and safety. This means that each person's questions and contributions are respected. When we feel safe and included, we can ask questions that will help us to understand the gospel. We can share insights and faith that might help someone else (see Romans 1:11–12).[62]

Many students clam up if they make a comment and the teacher doesn't acknowledge any validity to it or even rejects it because it wasn't what he or she was looking for. So a big part of making the classroom safe for comments is doing everything you can—within reason—to help students feel that their comments are respected. To start with, that means not making sarcastic or dismissive comments. But some comments are wacky or irrelevant enough that they'll test your patience.

So what do you do with that? What happens when students do give wrong answers?

First, look for any kernel of truth or applicability before

dismissing the answer. Then, even if it's a flat-out wrong answer to a factual question, let the student down gently by saying something like, "Not a bad guess." And not to beat a dead horse, but again, that's one of the reasons we much prefer open-ended questions to clear-cut factual questions. It's a lot easier to salvage even the most irrelevant answer to an open-ended question than it is with closed-ended, right-or-wrong, factual questions.

The second step is to acknowledge and build on their answers.

How do you do that?

Sometimes it's as simple as just saying thank you and nodding your head. It works best if you mean it. Often we'll restate part of a student's answer and build on it, both for the sake of letting the student know we understood and appreciated his of her point and for the sake of emphasis to help the rest of the class get the point. We can even honor a question by asking a follow-up question that draws further insights: "That's an interesting point, Alan. Just how would sharing the gospel with your friends now better prepare you to serve as a full-time missionary?" Finally, as students, we know our comments have been appreciated when teachers refer to them later in the lesson to summarize or reiterate a point.

But what about irrelevant comments? I hate it when people give an answer that doesn't relate at all to the question.

Validation still works if you can find any truth to the comment, even if it was unrelated to the question. We know a high priest group instructor who had a man in his group who would frequently interject absolutely irrelevant comments. Finally, the teacher started making a game of trying to find ways to relate this brother's off-the-wall comments to his lesson. So one day the teacher was giving a lesson about the Restoration, and this brother raised his hand and said, "You know, we've got a big problem in this country: when the baby boomers die, there's not going to be enough room in our cemeteries to bury everyone. But I've got a solution—we should buy the top third of Canada and move our old cemeteries there." Seriously.

What on earth do you do with a comment like that?

We'd probably be at a loss too, but this good teacher said something like, "You know, sometimes we really have to think out of the box like that to solve hard problems. And maybe that's why the Lord used a young, humble man like Joseph Smith—because he didn't think he had all the answers already."

It won't usually be that difficult, but if you look hard enough, you can usually find something to affirm in students' answers, even when their points don't really relate to the question. The truth is, you'll be surprised at how many good points your students make. And they will notice and remember when later in the lesson you mention a phrase they used, especially if you nod to them to let them know you've remembered their point and are reiterating it.

I've noticed some students rarely participate. What can I do to draw in those kinds of students?

A friend once admitted that he'd really like to participate in the discussion in our ward's Gospel Doctrine class more. "Some people seem to have no lag time between when a question is asked and when a good answer comes into their brain," he said. "For me, it takes about thirty seconds. So a lot of the time when the teacher asks a question, I come up with a good answer thirty seconds later—after the class has already moved on."

One simple way to involve more people is to give students as much advance notice of the question as possible. There are a bunch of ways you can do this, but the bottom line is that the more time you can give between first asking the question and asking for an answer, the more time people will have to come up with an answer. There are plenty of people in every class like our friend—people who have great insights but have a hard time articulating an answer instantaneously.

So how do you give people time to formulate their answers?

One simple principle is to ask questions *before* reading a verse or watching a video clip.[63] For example, when we're teaching the story of Balaam, the Old Testament prophet who falls, we may want the students to draw some lessons about compromising their standards to get worldly gain. So we might introduce the story by saying, "This story is a lot of fun, because it's got a talking donkey. But it's actually quite valuable as a parable for our own lives. As we read Balaam's story together, think about what it teaches us about the temptations we face to compromise our principles." That kind of invitation helps because it gives students more time to come up with an answer to the question you'll eventually ask, and it also focuses their thoughts and helps them get more out of the scriptural passage.

Another great technique is to ask people to discuss a particular question with the person sitting next to them. Rob initially resisted this approach because it just seemed too old-school. But he's come to embrace it and now uses it regularly in his classes at BYU—Idaho. The fact is that the same class that may sputter when asked a question as a whole usually erupts into conversation when asked to discuss the same question in pairs.

I don't see how that's giving people any more notice. It's just shrinking the size of the class.

That's true for the two minutes we give students to discuss a question with their partners. But when we then ask the same question to the class as a whole, everyone's had a chance not only to formulate an answer, but also to articulate it to a partner. We almost never have a slow discussion following an exercise in which students discuss a question with a partner.[64]

An extreme version of the notice idea is to ask students, either collectively or individually, to think about a certain question a day or week in advance. While she was serving as a Gospel Doctrine teacher, Mark's wife put a note on the board below the next week's reading assignment of Abraham 1–2 and Genesis 12–17: "Bring one question that you have related to the Abrahamic Covenant." It gave her students advance notice of the subject and also gave them something to look for in their reading, something to possibly answer, and some input into at least a portion of the next class discussion.

Teachers might announce at the end of class that for tomorrow's lesson they'd love to hear some students' stories about how the priesthood has blessed their lives. Or they might slip notes to individual students asking them to come prepared to share a few thoughts on a particular topic. This allows students to come up with stories or comments that might not come to them in the spur of the moment. That's the same rationale behind journaling, which really fits in here under the heading of giving students time to come up with answers. But we find that technique so effective that we'll discuss it in a chapter all its own.

Mark observed a teacher prepare students with this simple warning: "I've got three levels of questions coming. The first is an easier question, and the second two are a bit more difficult." Then the teacher turned on the overhead projector. There was a paper covering the overhead. The teacher revealed the first question and asked, "Who'd like an easy one?" Several students who wouldn't normally participate jumped on the question. Others seemed to hold back, waiting for the challenge of the more difficult questions. When the teacher revealed questions two and three, a completely different group of students responded. The entire class seemed to step up.

Another simple technique some teachers use is to slow things down just a bit by rephrasing or elaborating on a question after throwing it out. Sometimes teachers ask a question and get an answer right away, but if they don't, explaining the question a little more gives people extra time.

For example?

In a lesson about Balaam, a teacher's first cut at the question might simply be, "So what does this story teach us about selling out?" But if this doesn't get a response, the teacher might explain a bit and ask the question another way: "Balaam has a prophetic gift, and he starts out by refusing to misuse it. But then he decides to visit the wicked king, still insisting that he'll only say what the Lord wants him to say. But in the end, we learn that he caves in. Is there a moral to this story that we can learn from? How are we sometimes tempted to sell out spiritually?" By elaborating on the question and rephrasing it, the teacher has given the students more time to think about their answers and has made the question clearer. And even those students who don't share their answers out loud benefit from trying to come up with one.

How?

The very process of coming up with answers and insights helps us learn, even if we don't share the answers. Still, students do learn more when they share their answers, which is why we'll sometimes call on students. Of course, then it's especially important to give them some notice that we'll be calling on them.

What do you mean? Do you tell them before class?

No, but you can put their name *before* a question, or you could say, "Patricia, could you read verse . . . ? Afterward, Brock will share some thoughts about it."

Do you really think it's right to call on students? What if they're uncomfortable commenting? Don't you risk scaring them away from your class if you call on people?

You do have to be careful, and once you've got the level of participation you want from all the students in the class, you may decide not to call on anyone who doesn't volunteer. But getting to that level almost always involves calling on people at some point.

But what about agency? Shouldn't students be allowed to decide when they want to participate?

For that reason, we prefer to narrow things down to a small group in hopes of getting a student to volunteer. We might call on a row or just the boys or someone who's lived in a different state before or someone who is a convert. It changes the dynamic. Sometimes if a teacher has put a question to the whole class, it takes a lot of gumption for students to raise their hands. Some students may even feel like they're showing off. But if you've limited your question to a specific group of students, it's remarkable how quickly people will come forward with comments.

Another useful technique is to ask for an answer from someone who hasn't had a chance to comment yet. That will help broaden participation if you've got a few students dominating the discussion.

It opens the question up to other people and subtly sends the message to those who've been dominating the discussion that they may need to give others a chance to answer more questions. We might even list two or three individuals who haven't talked much and ask one of them to answer.

Finally, if we do single out an individual, we might do it in a good-natured way that allows them to pass on the opportunity if they choose—saying something like, "Allison, did you have something to add here? It looks like you've got a thought worth sharing." Here's a note we received from a student on the shy side whom we prodded periodically in just that way: "I like that you call on me and encourage me to speak up. You tend to do it when I actually have something to say and I just don't realize it."

Once you manage to get students like that to participate successfully, they're much more likely to volunteer an answer later in class. That's why it's so important to make it a safe and successful experience for them when you call on them. We never call on students to single them out—unless they're really messing around and other techniques haven't worked. (We'll discuss that more in our chapter on discipline.) Basically, we try to be very careful about calling on students so they don't have a bad experience. Still, calling on students directly is sometimes the only way to help them climb over the barriers to participation, after we've lowered those barriers in all the other ways we can.

Any other keys to asking questions well?

Get students to elaborate on their answers. Pull more out of them. Sometimes we see teachers who are so happy to get an answer at all that they quickly move on. But there's often a lot more behind the students' answers, and some of the best comments we've gotten over the years have come from follow-up questions.

So how do you draw them out more?

A few simple phrases usually do the trick—stuff like, "Tell me more about that," or "Excellent—why?" With the right students we might even challenge their answers just a bit, but always in a safe way that won't undermine their testimony. "Is it really so important to read the scriptures *every* day? Why not read three times as much every third day?" Great teachers use questions much like great conversationalists do: they listen to answers and build on them with more questions.[65]

Okay, one last question. Sometimes I ask a question, and no one says a thing. It's so awkward. How do you deal with that?

Ride it out. Silence is not necessarily golden, but it's not your enemy or even a sign of failure. Because most of us aren't used to silent gaps in conversation, we feel uncomfortable with them. So if we ask a question and no one answers right away, we quickly move on.

And instead we should savor the silence?

We're not saying that we should savor it so much as that we shouldn't let it scare us away. Try rephrasing and restating the question first, but then if no one answers, be willing to let the class be silent for a few seconds. Doing so can provide what Elder Maxwell called "moments of deliberate pause,"[66] moments that allow students to reflect and the Spirit to work on their hearts. Besides, when teachers move on too quickly, students know they can avoid answering questions by just keeping their mouths closed for a couple of seconds. Especially when you're trying to create a culture of participation where past teachers have just lectured, you may need to ride out some awkward silences before students will participate. And if the question is good, a lot of good can be happening in the minds and hearts of students as they process the question in the silence.

Giving Notice

Ask questions before reading or watching.

Have students discuss questions in pairs.

Plant questions in advance.

Restate questions and elaborate.

Call on students by name or small group before asking the question.

- Start early.
- Make the classroom safe.
- Give as much notice as possible.
- Draw students out with follow-up questions.
- Ride out the silence.

TEN

TESTIMONIES WITHOUT MICROPHONES

In 2003, CES introduced a teaching emphasis that, among other things, invited seminary and institute teachers to "help students learn how to explain, share and testify of the doctrines and principles of the restored gospel. We are to give them opportunities to do so with each other in class." Nothing helps students experience the Spirit more than testifying or hearing other students testify. "Faith-promoting incidents occur in teaching," Elder Robert D. Hales has observed, "when students take a role in teaching and testifying to their peers."[67] In fact, we'd call this the crowning principle of participation. And the more natural the context and the more genuine the need we can create for testifying, the more easily the testimonies will flow.

Are you saying I should hold a weekly testimony meeting?

No. Testimony meetings are great, but we don't need a testimony meeting or a microphone to bear a testimony. Too often we think of testimonies only as statements we make in fast and testimony meeting that begin with, "I'd like to bear my testimony," and include all the essential elements of a true testimony. Yet some of the best testimonies we've heard didn't even include the word *testimony.* There's often great power when people testify without microphones, whether it's during class discussions, family home evenings, conversations with children in the car, or even bishop's interviews.

Rob remembers when, as a bishop, he started interviewing young children for temple recommends for the broadcast of the Nauvoo Temple dedication and a couple of other temple dedications. Frankly,

he wasn't quite sure what to ask nine-year-olds in that kind of inter-
view. Some of the usual language seemed over their heads. So one of
the questions he asked these children was whether they thought the
Church was true. They always said they did, which was no surprise.
But then Rob followed up by asking how they knew the Church was
true. It was amazing what wonderful answers these children gave.
None of them used the word *testimony* in their answers, but they testified powerfully as they explained from their hearts how they had felt
the Spirit or seen the fruits of the gospel in their lives. It was great.

Mark has had similar experiences in interviewing eight-year-old
children for baptism. When asked a question like, "Why do you want
to get baptized?" children often explain gospel principles in simple
and yet profound detail. They respond to questions like, "How can
receiving the Holy Ghost help you?" or "What will be required of you
once you join Jesus' church?" with a spirit of testimony and conviction, even at this early age.

**Maybe I'm living in another universe, but I'm having a hard time
believing that the teenagers in my class will voluntarily bear their
testimonies. Maybe that works at an extraordinary event like
youth conference, but Sunday School? That's a whole different
matter. I'm not sure how many of these kids even have testimonies.**

Students often find testimonies while bearing them.

**So just throw the kids in the deep end of the pool, hoping they'll
learn how to swim?**

Not quite. It's more like working with swimming students who have
actually learned a lot about swimming but have been relying on kick-
boards the whole time and don't realize how well they actually know
how to swim. When Brigham Young called Junius Wells to be the first
Young Men president in the Church, he suggested that Brother Wells
start at the top of the roll and give each young man an opportunity to
bear his testimony until he had worked his way through the whole roll.
We don't advocate that exact approach, but President Young's explanation for having the young men speak says a lot about why giving youth

an opportunity to bear their testimony is so important. He said, "More people have obtained a testimony while standing up trying to bear it than down on their knees praying for it."[68] And he's right.

Many young missionaries have wondered whether they really have testimonies. But once they start opening their mouths and hearts and begin talking about whatever conviction they think they have, they find that they have testimonies and that their testimonies are growing. President Packer described that very process in his marvelous talk about the workings of the Spirit called "The Candle of the Lord":

> It is one thing to receive a witness from what you have read or what another has said; and that is a necessary beginning. It is quite another to have the Spirit confirm to you in your bosom that what *you* have testified is true. . . . Oh, if I could teach you this one principle. A testimony is to be *found* in the *bearing* of it! . . . It is the moment when you have gone to the edge of the light and stepped into the darkness to discover that the way is lighted ahead for just a footstep or two. . . . To speak out is the test of your faith.[69]

In terms of spiritual growth, that is one of the most valuable things about a mission: it gives missionaries daily opportunities to bear their testimonies, and in the process they discover that they really do have testimonies. And the more they share them, the more their testimonies grow. That's exactly why great teachers try to create opportunities for students to do more than just listen or even just answer factual or analytical questions. They create situations where students end up bearing their testimonies, often without the students even realizing they're doing so.

We think that's exactly what Elder Scott was hoping would happen when he urged us to give students more opportunities to teach.

What? Have them teach the whole lesson?

Not necessarily, and probably not often. Instead, whether we assign them the daily devotional in seminary or just ask them in

advance to talk about a specific principle in class, we've found that
Elder Scott's "simple four-step outline" works really well: He asked
that we have students state the principle or doctrine, give an example
from real life to illustrate it, support it with a scripture, and then
share a personal testimony and application of the principle.[70] We've
had great results in asking students to do this.

**I like that, but give me more. How do you get students to open
up and speak from the heart?**

Before answering that directly, we should note that a big part of it
is paving the way.

What do you mean?

Establishing rapport, using great Openers, asking good questions—
all these things help create an environment where students can and do
participate. It's crucial that students feel comfortable letting their
voices be heard in class. It's virtually impossible for a new teacher to
successfully begin a class by trying to elicit testimonies. But if you've
invested time getting to know students and drawing them out and
getting some thoughtful discussions going, then you've laid the
groundwork for the most important kind of participation.

**Fair enough. Once you've done all that, though, how do you get
students to bear testimonies without microphones?**

With great questions. Great questions elicit testimonies.

That's it?

It was simple questions that got the children in those interviews
to share their testimonies. "Why do you think this is Jesus' church?"
or "What makes you think that?" With the right kind of question, a
good teacher invites testimonies. Any number of basic patterns will
work for these kinds of questions: "How do you feel about . . . ?" or
"How do you know that . . . ?" or "Why is it so important that we . . . ?"
or "How has (fill in the doctrinal blank) blessed your life?" In crafting
these kinds of questions, just ask yourself whether the answer to the

question is likely to prompt students to speak from the heart and to share their spiritual convictions. If it does, it's a good question—for this purpose, anyway. Remember, this is the crowning principle of participation. Other kinds of questions play other important roles, like helping students glean truths from the scriptures or helping them explain those truths to others.

One other technique we have found to be very helpful in getting students to share the convictions of their hearts is role playing. Teachers might call up a student or two and pretend to be a friend who is struggling with a certain issue. The students' job is to shore up their friend, and they almost always bear testimony in the process—almost without realizing it.

We'll never forget the day when students played different roles from a New Testament story as we interviewed them on camera for a mock documentary. We actually had one student who was not a member, and we had asked her to be one of the disciples on the road to Emmaus. We'd given all the students a chance to read the appropriate passage of scripture, focusing on the role we were asking them to play. Then we'd ask questions. Some of them were basic, get-the-story-out kinds of questions. But then we asked the nonmember student, "So what did it feel like when you were walking with the Savior? How did you know it was Him?" Her response was amazing. Tears came to her eyes as she described how she thought these disciples must have felt. There's no doubt that she felt the Spirit as she gave that answer.

On another occasion we each decided to bring in some folks from our wards who were married to members but weren't members themselves. We assigned the students portions of the plan of salvation and supporting scriptures and gave them time to prepare in advance. Then we had them teach the guests, and we encouraged the guests to ask genuine questions.

How'd they do? That sounds kind of scary.

It was, but our students did remarkably well. But when one of our first classes didn't seem to testify enough, we tried something with our later classes that really helped. Just before they began teaching, we told them to make sure the guest not only understood what they believed, but *how they felt* about it.

And?

And the difference was astonishing. Not once did they say, "I'd like to bear my testimony." But their teaching and their answers to the investigators' questions were laced with testimony. As a result, the Spirit had a strong presence there. The students felt it and our guests felt it. It was wonderful.

What about when Gospel Doctrine teachers ask people to share specific experiences, like a time when their prayers have been answered? It seems like they're trying to do what you say, but a lot of times it doesn't really work. Their questions are just followed by an awkward silence.

Asking those kinds of questions is a good idea, and sometimes it works. But there are a couple of things we've found that make that kind of request work better. The first is to plant a request or several requests in advance. You can whisper the request to a student or two at the beginning of class, or better yet, give them a note or a phone call the day before. For example, if we were teaching about miracles in the book of Moroni, we might give a student a note telling her that we were going to be discussing miracles tomorrow and asking her to be prepared to share some ways in which she has seen miracles in her life or in her family. Or if we know a student has had some relevant experiences, we might be more specific with our request. If we know a student has helped a friend join the Church, we'll tell him we're going to be discussing sharing the gospel and we'll ask him if he would share his feelings about the experience.

What if they can't come up with an experience or they're not willing to share it?

Good gospel teachers try to avoid putting students on the spot unnecessarily, so they often ask a few people in advance and don't call on any of them by name. They might try to make eye contact when they ask for people to share experiences. Often, that's enough. It's amazing how much more willing people are to share personal experiences if they're given some time to think about them in advance.

The next chapter discusses another particularly effective way to give the entire class a bit of advance notice so they can gather their thoughts and then share their experiences about a principle and testify of it.

- No microphone is necessary.
- Students often find testimonies while bearing them.
- Use great questions to elicit testimonies.
- Role-play.

ELEVEN

WRITING THINGS DOWN TO OPEN STUDENTS UP

To be honest, neither of us was much for taking notes in class during high school or college. But we've become so convinced of the importance of recording certain spiritual thoughts that we now hate to attend a gospel meeting or class without having a pen and paper in hand. And as teachers, we've discovered that we can use writing to help students not only remember important truths, but also discover them and share them with others. In this chapter we explore why writing things down can help students open up—and how to use writing effectively.

Actually, I'm not much one for writing things down. I prefer to make mental notes. What's the big deal with having students write stuff down?

There are a number of benefits to taking notes in any class. Before discussing those benefits, though, it may help to describe the different situations in which we encourage our students to write.

But first we should mention that there are many different ways to encourage students to take notes. Mark provides his seminary students with spiral notebooks at the beginning of each school year. He then bases part of students' grades on filling up a certain number of pages in their "journal" each semester—a simple but effective way to get them to use the notebooks. Although Rob doesn't grade students on the contents of their in-class notebooks, he does let them know that there will be a final exam and that they'll probably do better on it if they take good notes in class. He also requires students to submit weekly journals in which they record insights from their study of the scriptures. But these grade-based reasons for writing only get you so far, and they're not available to most gospel teachers. As with participation, we find that an even more effective way to get students to write is to spend some time at the beginning of the semester or the new Gospel Doctrine year helping them see the benefits of taking notes and recording impressions.

Wait a minute. You're not suggesting using journals with adult students, are you?

Whether students are children or adults, a willingness to take notes suggests a willingness to learn. Rob will never forget the comment made by the wife of a visiting General Authority after a missionary zone conference. She complimented the missionaries on the fact that so many of them were taking notes. "It makes it clear that you don't think you know everything already," she said, as well as Rob can recollect. "Taking notes shows you believe there's something you can learn from us." Being prepared to take notes in class sends that very message not just to the teacher, but to the Lord.

It's probably easier to encourage this in a college religion class, where students may be taking notes in other classes as well. But Mark's wife has been a Gospel Doctrine teacher twice. Both times she purchased spiral notebooks for the class members and helped them learn the power of writing. (On the practical side of things, spiral notebooks invariably go on sale at "back to school" time for a nominal cost. There's typically some budget money available to cover a small cost like this.)

We've seen Primary teachers of eight- and nine-year-olds use journals and writing as well. It's really transferable to most teaching in the Church. And as students practice writing simple things or even copying quotes from a chalkboard, they get practice and can easily become better at using their journals as a tool for communication with the Spirit.

You mentioned different situations in which you have students take notes. What are they?

First, we encourage students to copy quotes, scripture chains, and other critical points from each class. We're amazed at how many students will write something in their journals whenever we say, "You might want to write that down" or "I've noted that cross-reference in my margin." We hope they'll get to the point, like many attentive adult students, where they'll highlight things in their scriptures and write down scripture chains or quotes without any prodding from us. But if we can help get them started by coming right out and suggesting they do it, we're happy to help.

Along these same lines, every so often as we prepare the lesson we'll find a quote that we feel is really pertinent to the lesson. We'll shrink it down and make copies for everyone. When we're ready to use it, we pass it out during the lesson and then read it together and discuss it. Then rather than having the handout thrown away or put somewhere that it will be forgotten, we have the students paste it into their journals using glue sticks. They can write a reference by the side of it and some notes that remind them of our discussion and application for it.

It's a way to get them thinking of their journals as a great resource, a great place to record good quotes as well as important thoughts of their own. For instance, when someone has just made an insightful comment, we might say something like, "Wow, that was a great comment. That sounds journal-worthy to me." It's surprising how many kids will make a note in their journals about it. The more teachers suggest writing things down, the more things students will write down.

Finally, you can also use a journal as a summary for the lesson. We'll sometimes ask a question like this: "If you were to summarize our lesson in one sentence that we could all record in our journals, what would you say?" We'll get two or three comments, and 90 percent of the kids will be writing these thoughts in their journals. You can also do it the other way around, where you give students time to write a summary statement of the lesson and then call on two or three students to share their ideas with the class. It's kind of like the summary charts in this book—some simple things to remember so that you can retain and apply what you've learned.

All these techniques basically involve students writing down what others have said. That might be the lowest level of writing, but it helps students get in the habit of writing in their journals.

If this is the lowest level of writing, what are the higher levels?

Beyond getting students to transfer ideas from the blackboard to their notebooks, we want them to get ideas and feelings from their minds and hearts into their notebooks. So periodically, we'll ask questions aimed to help students apply gospel principles to their lives, and then we'll give them time to record their thoughts.

How does having students write in journals square with the idea of increasing student participation? Having students quietly write things down seems like the opposite of having them raise their hands and make comments.

Getting students to write can actually be one of the most powerful tools to increase student participation.

How?

First, not all participation has to be students making comments out loud to the entire class. When students write down thoughts in response to a question, they're "virtually participating." And instead of just one student speaking at a time, with many students not speaking at all, nearly every student in the class will start writing when we ask one of these questions. In two minutes, all of the students in the class have been able to participate and articulate their thoughts, even though they didn't do it out loud.

Really? I'd think some students would just sit there and not write.

That may be true at first, but over time and with a little prodding, we get most of our students to write regularly in response to application questions. It helps to walk around the room and glance at students' papers while they write; it sends a message to class members who aren't trying that you really do expect them to write. We've seen many a student pick up his or her pencil as we've approached.

What kinds of questions work best for this sort of journal exercise?

The key is to ask yourself the question, "What do I want to have happen in the lives of my students?" For example, if your hope in teaching about David and Goliath is that your students will come away with more faith to battle the giant problems in their lives, focusing on that objective will help you create great questions to facilitate it in your students' lives. And it doesn't have to be a single question, although you want a great question to begin with. You can periodically follow up with related questions as students are writing.

Can you give me some examples?

If we were teaching the Book of Mormon, in the first few chapters we might start with a simple exercise to lower the barriers of entry. We might have students list Laman and Lemuel at the top of the page on one side and Nephi on the other. Then we could ask them to list some phrases from 1 Nephi that described each of the brothers. Later we might ask a more thought-provoking application question like this: "Lehi gave up everything and 'dwelt in a tent' because that's what the Lord wanted. Write about some of the sacrifices the Lord expects us to make today."

What if they're stumped? What if they just can't come up with anything?

That's where the follow-up questions and comments come in handy. "To obtain a land of promise, Lehi and his family had to move, leaving behind friends and a house and property. What kinds of things does God expect us to give up to reach our personal lands of promise? What about habits? Selfish ambitions? The wrong kinds of friends?" We'll often provide 10 or 15 seconds between questions in a series geared to help them answer the first question. We've seen how some of the follow-up questions have sparked thoughts and caused kids who had been stuck before to start writing.

We should mention one other technique that really seems to help students loosen up and write down their feelings: playing music. It's surprising what a difference it makes to play some appropriate music while students write—especially teenagers. It invites the Spirit and sort of creates a soundtrack for their thoughts. It also frames a time limit around the writing assignment so that we can move on to other things in the limited class time.

Do you do journal exercises like this during every class?

We hope students will write a little something every time. But we don't include a writing assignment during every class. During our daily seminary classes, we'd typically give formal prompts once or twice a week to try to keep them in the habit of writing often.

Inviting students to write about these kinds of questions helps accomplish many of the things we've talked about in our other chapters. It's a great way to draw out personal application. And it really facilitates their learning by the Spirit and receiving and recognizing customized promptings for their lives. But in our experience, one of the greatest benefits has been with discussion.

It does sound like a great tool, but I'm not sure I see how it facilitates discussion.

Remember the chapter about asking questions? We emphasized the point that students often need time to formulate a good answer. And when the teacher moves on after getting an answer or two to a question, many students are left behind without having a chance to ponder or respond to something that might otherwise have been a spiritual moment. Journal exercises are a great way to provide some time for students to reflect and collect their thoughts and feelings before sharing them with the class. We've noticed that giving students this kind of time to collect their thoughts is particularly helpful when it comes to getting students to testify.

For instance, Mark remembers asking students to share an example of a time when they ended up actually enjoying service that they'd initially done begrudgingly. They looked at him blankly for 15 seconds. So he shifted gears and asked them to pull out their journals. He gave them the same question, but this time he allowed them time to ponder it. Within a few seconds virtually every student in the class was writing. When they were done, he was able to ask the same question and get very good responses from almost everyone in the class.

So do you always follow a journal exercise like this with a discussion?

Not always—sometimes we run out of time. And the exercise of writing is valuable all by itself because students end up with a recorded testimony. But when we invite students to share some of their thoughts, it gives them an opportunity to testify with power in a nonthreatening way.

Do they just read what they wrote?

Occasionally, but not usually. We might say something like, "If it's not too personal [always a good qualifier], it would bless all of us if some of you would share your thoughts or feelings with the rest of us." You'll get some volunteers who will read their entry or paraphrase what they have recorded, but most will speak from their hearts, with the advantage of having had time to reflect on the question in advance. Having something written in front of them in case they need it is like a security blanket; it gives students confidence, especially those who are reluctant to participate in class.

One other participation benefit of these kinds of exercises is that it gives teachers a chance to scan the students to see which ones seem most engaged in the writing. As you glance around the room at papers, you can tell from how much students have written which ones are more likely to have something to say. We feel more comfortable calling on students we know have just written several thoughts about the question we're answering.

That sounds like the highest level to me, but you said you used writing in three different kinds of situations. What's the other scenario where you have students write?

It's not really a scenario where we have them write or where they write anything we tell them to write. That's what makes it the highest level of writing. It's where they write down something they feel prompted to do or become—a customized prompting of the Spirit.

A few years ago, Mark heard a talk by Elder Richard G. Scott entitled "Helping Others to Be Spiritually Led."[71] For him it was one of those moments where he felt the Spirit hit him hard, and he knew he needed to start doing what Elder Scott challenged him to have his students do: "Were I a teacher of young students, I would have them commit to apply this principle: I will seek to learn by what I hear, see, and feel. I will write down the things I learn and will do them."[72] Elder Scott wasn't just talking about learning things the teacher taught. He explained, "You will find that as you write down precious impressions, often more will come. . . . *What you write down from the impressions you feel will be the most valuable help you can receive.*"[73]

If you've received the prompting already, why does it really matter if you write it down?

That brings us to benefits, and we'll take them in the reverse order of the types of note taking we just described. We can forget promptings of the Spirit, just like we can forget appointments and birthdays and other things we plan to do. Writing promptings down helps us remember them so that we can act on them.

When Mark heard Elder Scott charge students to write down the things they felt and to do them, it pierced Mark to the center. He knew that this would be a valuable tool, not only for his students and his teaching, but in his own personal life as well. So he began to keep a journal—a "revelation record," as one of his colleagues calls it, where he could write impressions of the Spirit as they came while he studied the scriptures. In doing so, Mark discovered that Elder Scott's promise held true: He found that as he recorded his "precious impressions," more came.[74] Having learned for himself the value of recording spiritual insights, Mark was then in a position to teach his students to do the same thing.

Okay, I can see that working for you, but does it really work with students?

Yes. We've chosen to illustrate some of the benefits of journal writing with five students' comments that are quite representative of what many of our students share with us about journaling.[75] The comments from this high school senior highlight a second benefit of writing down the feelings we receive from the Spirit:

> Journal writing has become more important to me throughout the years as I have looked back and read things I was inspired to write years ago. Some journal pages were accidentally thrown out, and the idea of not being able to refer back to them taught me how important it is to keep records of spiritual experiences, so I will remember them and remember how much the Lord blesses me and to be reminded that the Lord answers my prayers. And the more records of this that I have, the less I can deny it on a rainy day. It is almost like a spiritual savings account, the oil in my lamp.

Along those same lines, another student said that her classroom journal was "like a personal journal in that you can look back and remember every day how you felt."

Just as we tend to forget the actions the Spirit prompts us to take, we can also forget the witnessing and comforting feelings the Spirit gives us. So a second benefit of recording the feelings of the Spirit in a journal is that when we are basking in the light of the Spirit, we can testify to ourselves on that future "rainy day" when we might otherwise forget the spiritual confirmation we once had. Writing down what we feel from the Spirit helps us combat the spiritual Alzheimer's that afflicts people of all ages.

Another related benefit is that the very process of writing down feelings builds testimonies as students recognize the Spirit and understand the principles that are being taught. Here's what one high school junior wrote:

> I find that as I write down things that I think or hear, I am able to better understand and remember those things. Although I don't do it very often it has helped me to express my feelings and strengthen my testimony by doing so.

A freshman echoed these sentiments:

> My testimony has grown a lot from writing. I do not write in my journal at home and only write here in class. Even just writing in class has increased my testimony. I write my thoughts down and promptings from the Spirit. Writing stuff down helps me to know that I believe what I am writing because I only write what I believe. Writing stuff down helps me reminisce about times I went through before. I can go back and look at what I have previously written. I also write down what I would most likely forget because sitting down and writing forces me to think about what I have learned. I know I should write at home, but I am just too lazy to get it out and do it.

A comment from another freshman underscores the practical benefits of collecting quotes and noting principles in a single, secure place:

> Having a journal for seminary is an ingenious idea. There are so many different uses for it. I've already used mine for a talk in sacrament meeting. There are those little quotes and bits of information that I know will be useful in the future.

Perhaps nothing sums up the benefits of having students write down impressions of the Spirit in a secure place better than this comment from a young woman:

> The blessings of writing promptings down [are] incredible. At EFY this past year I wrote down a lot of my feelings and understanding. A couple of weeks after I got back I read over some of the things I wrote. It amazed me how spiritual they were and how insightful some of the things were. Reading these things made me want to be as insightful as I was at EFY. So from then on I've wrote down my thoughts on the scriptures in my journal. So now when I have

questions I can just look back. And not always do I have the same impressions on a certain passage. It really depends on the day. I'll admit there are some days when I'm "too tired" and basically just go through the motions. But when I truly put my heart into it, it really blesses my life. When I write things down it seems to internalize easier and it's harder to forget. You'll always remember not only the [event] but you'll also remember the way you felt. And it makes you HAPPY. ☺

- Journals provide a great place for students to collect quotes, etc.
- Students can also summarize principles from the lesson in their journals.
- Responding in writing to thoughtful questions allows the entire class to participate virtually.
- Writing answers in journals prepares students to share answers with the class.
- Recording personal promptings helps students recognize and act on impressions from the Spirit.

TWELVE

VARIETY IN ALL THINGS

Just as a good cook doesn't serve the same meal every day, good teachers use variety to spice up their lessons. As a missionary, Mark ate macaroni and cheese at least four times a week for the first eight months of his mission. He hasn't eaten a complete serving since. In much the same way, when teachers use the same methods day after day, students become bored and disengaged. That's why great gospel teachers develop a good repertoire of techniques that can be used to create variety in the classroom.

Okay, but isn't there something good about a routine? Lots of kids respond well to structure.

Absolutely. We're all in favor of having some things happen every time you instruct. Seminary classes that have seating charts and daily devotionals as well as regular follow-up on scripture reading provide a stable, productive environment where lots of good things can happen. A Primary class where the teacher consistently takes a "roll call" of who brought their scriptures is a powerful way to reinforce the need to establish this habit. But part of the regular "routine" calls for a varied approach to teaching. You can have both structure in the class and variety in your teaching. In fact, using variety often adds to the order in the classroom.

Really? How?

Often, poor behavior in students is a sign of boredom. As we'll discuss more in the chapter about discipline, using variety to shift gears can help students who are starting to get restless. A transition from a lively activity done in pairs to a more contemplative writing exercise can calm a class and direct students to focus on the Spirit.

So the main purpose of variety is to control the students?

Order in the classroom is more of a by-product than the primary purpose of teaching with a variety of techniques.

So what's the main reason for using variety?

Variety makes the students want to be in your class. When teachers use many different techniques in their teaching, students tend to stay more focused. Mixing up the way we teach helps keep students a bit more on the edge of their seats. And as our lessons inspire curiosity in our students, students ask more questions and take more responsibility in the learning process. In short, variety helps draw students in and keeps them coming back.

Is that it? It seems like you could keep them coming back with candy if you needed to.

Variety does much more than just engage students. When we use variety, we are more open to the promptings of the Spirit than if we find ourselves firmly entrenched in the same way of doing things every day.

Consider missionaries. If they use the same approach at every door, it's often difficult for them to recognize and respond to a prompting from the Spirit to say something that will meet the unique needs of a particular individual. If missionaries have decided in advance to talk about the Book of Mormon at every single door, they might not be receptive to a prompting from the Spirit to discuss life after death when they knock on the door of a man whose wife recently died. Using several different door approaches makes it easier for missionaries to be receptive to promptings from the Holy Ghost to customize the door approaches to meet the needs of each individual.

The same is true for gospel teaching in the classroom. One day Rob was sitting down to prepare a lesson for 3 Nephi 17 in his usual way. He prayerfully prepared a rather extensive outline for class. But as the time for class approached, he felt a fairly specific prompting not to use the outline, other than one short story to introduce the chapter. He felt impressed to play some music while giving students time to read the whole chapter and then to invite as many of them as possible to share one insight from the chapter. It was counterintuitive, and he almost didn't heed the prompting. But because he had been willing to try a variety of approaches in the past, he was perhaps more sensitive to that prompting than he would have been if he were in a comfortable rut of doing things the same way each day. And it proved to be his best class of the semester.

Many of our best classes happen when we take an inspired detour from the usual way of doing things. And when we regularly mix up the way we teach, we're more open to promptings to take such inspired detours.

I worry about using certain techniques because I know that some of my students don't like them. In fact, I'm not sure that any single technique will ever work for all my students.

That's all the more reason to use a variety of techniques. Part of our commitment to variety stems from a fundamental belief that different students learn in different ways. When we rely largely on one or two teaching methods, we might connect well with some of our students but completely miss the mark with others. For instance, one of Mark's strengths is telling stories. It's a powerful tool, but when overused it becomes too centered on the teacher and borders on lecturing. As we discussed in the chapters on participation, even the best lecturers or storytellers don't meet the needs of some of their students, particularly those who are visual learners. Teachers armed with an arsenal of different teaching techniques are better able to meet the needs of students who come with a variety of preferred learning styles.

Many students are visual learners—people who just need to see something written out or diagrammed to really have it distill upon them. Mark remembers trying to teach a seminary class about chiasmus—a Hebrew literary style in which parallel ideas are repeated in an inverted way and often point to a central message. No matter how many times he explained this form of poetry, some students just couldn't grasp it—until he finally diagrammed it on the board. With the diagram, all of the students understood what chiasmus was and why it was important.

So how do I get more variety in my teaching? I just don't think I can do something like role plays, or whatever you use to create variety.

Teachers who are committed to having variety in their lessons have to be committed to trying new things—and occasionally failing. And as with participation, teachers who try to increase the variety in their lessons and come up short will be tempted to slip back into safe mode to avoid any failures. Without a real commitment to creating some variety in their lessons, teachers often find themselves teaching their lessons the same way every time.

With role playing, for example, Mark observed Rob develop his ability to use this particular technique. Although Mark felt Rob's first attempts were good, it was very educational to watch him improve over time.

How'd he improve?

Through trial and error, Rob discovered some techniques that worked better than others. For example, he found that students did better when playing roles from the scriptures if they had some time in advance to read the scripture passage in light of the role they'd be playing. He also discovered that when he hooked up a camera to a monitor so the students could see themselves on TV, the kids almost immediately became more focused and engaged. And when he played the role of a reporter himself, he discovered that he could move things along and keep the exercise more focused.

The point is that Rob was committed to using variety and making it work—even if some of the new techniques he tried didn't initially work as well as he hoped they would. To this day, Rob keeps a running list of changes he plans to make in the next semester, based on things that didn't go as well as he'd hoped during the current semester. When you try a new technique and it doesn't go well, simply evaluate how you can improve and then try it again. Getting back on the horse after being bucked off is part of a teacher's commitment to good teaching.

When striving for more variety, is anything out of bounds?

Variety itself is not the ultimate goal, so it's important to ask yourself a few things before trying a new technique aimed at increasing variety. Is it consistent with the Spirit and the subject? Does the technique support the content or distract from it? Frankly, some techniques that might be appropriate in helping students learn about Samson and Delilah aren't compatible with teaching about the Savior in Gethsemane. For example, playing "hot potato"—where students have to give a short answer before passing on an egg timer—is a great way to involve a lot of students quickly and cover a lot of ground. That makes it a great tool for discussing the missionary attributes of Ammon and his brethren, but not for teaching about the Atonement. The sacred nature of some subjects requires a particularly serious approach in order to avoid offending the Spirit. With each technique teachers consider, they should ask, "What should happen in the lives of those I teach as a result of this lesson?"[76]

Recognizing that I need to use techniques that match the message, how do I know if I have enough variety in any given lesson? I keep trying to diversify, but then I find myself slipping back into my usual routine or even new routines.

You may find it useful to incorporate a variety evaluation as the final step in your lesson preparation. You've considered the material carefully and prayed about the major principles you want to emphasize. You've also spent a fair amount of time crafting questions and considering how best to teach the principles on which you've focused. Now take a step back and look at how much variety you actually have in the techniques you're using. Half the battle in staying out of teaching ruts is recognizing that we're in them.

So every day I should come up with a mixture of different techniques. When I find a mixture that works, can I use that same formula every day?

That would be a great start, but even if you've built some variety into your routine, it still feels routine after a while. Think about the old *Donnie and Marie Show*. *Donnie and Marie* was a variety show—and there was plenty of variety in each episode. Unfortunately, it was almost always the same variety from show to show. Viewers soon knew when to expect a musical number with the guest, a figure-skating scene, and a pie in the face. Lessons with a variety of techniques can become just as predictable if we use the exact same package in the same order every day. That's why when we think of variety, we sometimes need to think beyond our individual lesson to what and how we've taught over several lessons.

About once or twice a semester, Rob has a day where he gives students two or three minutes to come up with an insight about a particular passage of scripture. He often directs each row to a slightly different chapter or passage in order to make sure the class covers the entire block of scriptures. Once students have had time to decide on an insight, he takes comments and occasionally builds on them. In the course of 50 minutes, he's sometimes able to elicit comments from all 48 students.

Used every day, this technique would get old. And it certainly doesn't allow for the in-depth understanding and application that can result from focusing our lesson on a couple of principles or doctrines. But once or twice a semester (especially early in the semester), it's a great way to help all the students in the class participate. And while using that single technique doesn't create much stylistic variety within that single lesson, it adds to the overall variety Rob's students experience during the semester.

When you talk about doing a variety audit of your lesson, it feels like you're completely focused on style rather than substance. Doesn't substance count for anything?

Absolutely. We hope our discussion of variety doesn't overshadow any of the things we've said earlier about substance. Teachers who don't master the content of what they teach but use a great variety of skills are like a marching band whose formations look great but whose music sounds terrible. For teachers, as for missionaries, getting the content right must come first: "Seek not to declare my word, but first seek to obtain my word, and then shall your tongue be loosed" (D&C 11:21). But while variety can never take the place of good content, it can help present good content in a more effective way.

All right, you've helped convince me that variety is important and shared some principles about how to inject more variety into my lessons. But I want specific ideas about different techniques I can use so that I can increase my repertoire. What have you got for me?

We almost hesitate to share a list of ideas like this, only because the list will certainly be incomplete. But we also understand the need to prime the pump. So we'll share a few things that have worked for us and might work for you under the right circumstances. Better yet, we hope these ideas inspire more of your own. Many of your best ideas will be sparked by someone or something else. Keeping a growing edge is more important than trying to mimic something you've seen in another class. We're firm believers that some of the greatest techniques have yet to be discovered.

With that caveat, here are a few of the techniques we sometimes use.

Varying who talks. Sometimes we have just one person talk, like when the teacher is telling a story or when someone is reading a scripture. Sometimes we have a few people talk, like when we're doing a role play or soliciting comments from students. These are the most common scenarios, so we find it useful to switch things up by occasionally having everyone talk and sometimes having no one talk.

That sounds chaotic.

We don't actually have them all talk at once in the same conversation. Instead, we invite students to discuss the same subject in pairs or small groups. And the room really does erupt in conversation.

What's the point of having no one talk?

Besides providing a nice calm after the storm, it's very useful to allow students some silence in which to ponder a question or record their thoughts in a journal, as discussed in the chapter about writing things down.

Okay, what else?

Stories. There's great power in illustrating a principle with a story, whether it's personal or from a Church magazine or even from a more ancient story. (Rob loves to tell the apocryphal story of Abraham busting up his father's idols and blaming it on the biggest idol.) Of course, it's important to be accurate and not to be self-promoting when using stories.

Find a favorite. When you want to cover several quotes or great scriptures, try creating a list or a handout and giving students a limited amount of time to choose a favorite. Each student can then prepare to share the quote or verse they chose, along with an explanation of why they liked it.

Questions. Rob has lately taken to requiring his classes to ask at least one question about the reading before he plunges into his lesson. The first question can be slow in coming, but it almost always triggers more. We've also given students time to come up with questions about particular passages of the reading. Mark has seen great success in asking students to write down one real-life question they have and then inviting them to scan a chapter for any insights into answering it.

Spotting patterns. To underscore a theme, we sometimes ask our students to underline or count all the occurrences of a word like *remember* or any variation of it in a particular passage (e.g., Helaman 5). Or we ask them to find wording that conveys a specific message, like phrases in the first half of John 1 that show that John knew Jesus was more than just a great teacher.

Scripture microscope. To show students just how much can be gleaned from the scriptures, Rob often begins his Book of Mormon classes by giving students two minutes to scrutinize 1 Nephi 1:1 to see if they can find any new insights. Invariably, he has to cut off the discussion after ten or fifteen minutes, even though the students have even more insights to share.

Scripture stories. While we want to spend the bulk of our time mining scripture stories for doctrines and principles, it's often necessary to review the basic plot of the stories. In addition to simply telling the story or having a student tell the story, we've used a variety of other techniques to accomplish this. One activity is to divide students into pairs and have one student tell the story from memory in as much detail as possible, with the other student getting a chance to add any missing details. Everyone then gets a chance to scan the story for any additional details (or answers to questions that inevitably arise when they tell the stories from memory). In a similar vein, we find that a challenging pretest about a story often heightens interest in the story itself.

Find a youth conference theme. Have students highlight and share phrases in the reading that would make a great youth conference theme with an explanation of why they chose that scripture.

Music. In addition to the musical opportunities we mentioned in our chapter about teaching with the Spirit, on occasion we've also invited students in advance to prepare a musical number relating to the lesson.

Visual aids and object lessons. The next chapter is entirely dedicated to a discussion of how pictures, slides of quotes, and other objects can help spice up a lesson and rivet students' attention.

Drawing or coloring pictures. This notion sounded silly to Rob when Mark first suggested it, but Rob was amazed to see some of the drawings students produced when invited to color a picture of Lehi's dream while the class simultaneously discussed 1 Nephi 8.

Videos and DVDs. The Church has produced some marvelous resources, and many of them seem to be underutilized. Short video clips from movies can be a great way to drive home a point. But movies should never be used as filler, so show only as much as you need to in order to make your point.

Newspaper articles and current events. When used judiciously, newspaper articles about current events can provide students with an opportunity to apply gospel doctrines to modern situations. Mark enjoys giving students a whole stack of newspapers or magazines with instructions to find pictures or headlines that apply to the principle he's teaching.

One of these things. Mark gets tremendous mileage out of a little takeoff on "one of these things doesn't belong" from *Sesame Street.* He puts four things together, three of which have some kind of obscure connection to each other and to the principle he wants to teach. Then the students guess which one doesn't belong and why, with some great discussion in the process. A variation on this is to find three or four things that all relate, but not in any clear way, like a dollar bill, an oil-burning lamp, and a key chain with an oil vial. When students finally connect the olive branches on the dollar bill with the olive oil in the lamp and the vial on the key chain, it's a great segue into a discussion about the many things an olive tree can represent.

Chalk for everyone. Mark has discovered that a quick way to generate discussion is to pose a question and then hand four or five students a piece of chalk with an invitation to write their answer on the board. Other students can line up for the chalk when they're ready, or those with the chalk can hand off the chalk to other students if there are no volunteers. The best questions for this exercise are broad ones for which answers can be short, like, "What are some of the biggest myths about repentance?" With a variety of statements, the teacher can then choose which ones to emphasize and expand on: "Someone wrote, 'It's easy.' Tell me more about what you meant with that, and why it's a myth."

Student teaching. We never give up the entire class to a single student, but we try to find ways to get them on their feet in front of the class to teach a principle, even if it's just for a few minutes. In seminary, devotionals at the beginning of class can be a great experience as long as the bar remains high. Rob has tried having one or two students briefly teach a concept of their choosing from the reading for the day in his classes at BYU—Idaho. Even group presentations can be productive: each group of four is charged with presenting an explanation of a principle, a supporting principle, a testimony of the principle, and a favorite verse or two from a hymn that illuminates the principle. In his missionary preparation classes, Rob occasionally tries an exercise where students write a one- or two-sentence statement of testimony or principle and then get a chance to stand at their seats and share their statements. We've also given students five minutes to prepare 60-second talks on a verse from the day's reading. The students then get a chance to give their 60-second talks. (We've found that some students are long-winded, so we sometimes create a contest with a prize for the student whose talk comes the closest to lasting exactly 60 seconds.) Whatever the method, nothing helps students learn a principle quite so well as having to explain it on their feet.

Role playing. We've had our students play everything from missionaries to parents of troubled youth to concerned friends. The more realistic the situation, the better the exercise. It's best when students can dig deep to explain and testify about gospel doctrines. Depending on the size of the class, we might first ask students to take turns role playing with each other and then try having one or two students participate in role playing in front of the entire class.

Miscellaneous. As we mentioned, we hesitated to share this list of ideas, lest it be viewed as limiting rather than inspiring. Many of our favorite techniques don't even appear on this list because it's too difficult to categorize them.

We'll share just one example of such a technique. In teaching King Benjamin's sermon on helping the poor in Mosiah 4, Mark wanted to have students understand that we are all beggars who need the mercy of the Lord. So he made a sign on a piece of cardboard that said, "Homeless and hungry. Will work for food." He showed it to the kids and asked for their reactions. He got a lot of opinions and stories about insincere beggars and scams. He probed further. "Do you think these beggars mean it when they say they will work for food?" He heard a wide range of "probably nots" and other such comments. Then he turned the piece of cardboard around to reveal a sign that said, "Will work for the celestial kingdom." He asked them if they ever "held up" this sign and if they really "meant it."

We discuss the importance of visual aids more completely in a later chapter, but the fact is that the cardboard sign was different enough that it really riveted students' attention. And the combination of what was on the front of the sign and what was on the back helped illuminate the principles taught in Mosiah 4 in a memorable way.

That's a great example, but it's also discouraging. I'm just not that creative, and I don't see how I can come up with ideas like that.

You can and you will. Once you understand why variety is so important and become committed to using it, you're well on your way. Your students' needs, the Spirit, and your talents will lead you to vary your teaching in edifying ways.

For those reluctant to plunge in and try to create variety using different techniques, Elder Maxwell has a great analogy:

> Someone once said to a hesitant, prospective wood-carver who didn't know quite how to begin, "Start making some chips!" Our first feeble attempts at creativity are often no more than that. But they are a beginning. Beauty and truth are all about us, beckoning us to respond. But perspiration usually precedes inspiration, and pondering, reverentially, almost always occurs before we make any breakthrough. Creative work is sweet, but it is work![77]

As you continually evaluate the purpose of your lessons and try to stay true to what the Spirit has prompted you to select as the principles to be taught, you'll discover plenty of ways to create variety in your lessons. Over time, your creative abilities will improve, as will your ability to create the proper balance among different kinds of techniques. In the end, there's really no limit to what you can create when you understand what you really want to have take place in the lives of your students and when you are willing to pay the price to involve them.

- Variety keeps students interested and engaged.
- Using a variety of techniques helps teachers remain flexible and open to the promptings of the Spirit.
- Using different techniques enables teachers to reach students with different learning styles.
- Being willing to experiment with different techniques—and occasionally failing—is essential to teaching with variety.
- All of our teaching techniques should be consistent with the Spirit and the subject matter.
- Review completed lesson plans to see how much variety you really have.
- Variety is simply a means to an end, not the ultimate aim of our teaching.

THIRTEEN
PICTURES AND POWERPOINT

We confess—we're guys. And that means that until computers came along, we hadn't fully discovered or embraced the power of visual aids in teaching. But now we understand much better just how helpful showing objects, pictures, and quotes can be—whatever the medium. We would have done well to pay more attention to the elaborate visual aid Moses instructed Joshua to use in teaching the children of Israel when they entered the promised land. With half the tribes standing on one mountain (Mount Gerizim) and the other half standing on another (Mount Ebal), the Levites read the blessings that would come to Israel from obeying God's law and the curses that would come to them from disobeying. After each curse, the tribes on Mount Ebal signaled their understanding by shouting, "Amen," and after each blessing, the tribes on Mount Gerizim presumably did the same (see Deuteronomy 27:11–26; Joshua 8:33–35). The result was what Elder Maxwell called a "great visual and choral panoply of teaching."[78] Surely, those Israelites could not pass by those two mountains again without being reminded of the stark choices before them and the vastly different consequences that would flow from their obedience or disobedience. Perhaps this is why at the end of his life Joshua chose Shechem (see Joshua 24:1)—nestled at the foot of these two mountains—as the place to offer his benedictory challenge, "Choose you this day whom ye will serve . . ." (Joshua 24:15).

Of course, particularly with modern technological innovations, there are dangers to using audiovisual tools. In this chapter, we discuss the advantages as well as the pitfalls of using visual aids to spice up your lesson.

Do you believe in using PowerPoint?

Before we start talking about exactly how to display them, let's just agree that visual images are powerful. As Elder Scott has observed, "Many students can capture a concept more easily visually than through the written word."[79] Seeing a picture of the prophet helps us visualize him more than simply hearing the phrase "the prophet" does. When we display an image, it can stimulate what we call "productive daydreaming." Whether it's a replica of the brass plates or the Liahona or a bow or a candle or a loaf of bread, when we display an image for the students to see during a whole segment of the lesson, we can sometimes see students' eyes come back to the image throughout the lesson. It draws them into the story or principle we're discussing.

The same is true for quotes. Read a quote—even slowly—and it sinks in with a relatively small percentage of the class. But read a quote and display it for a while, and that percentage goes up dramatically. When we simply read a quote, maybe one student in a hundred will ask us for a copy of the quote after class. But when we display a quote on the board or on the screen, many students will copy it down, even without our suggesting that they do. It gives people time to let the quote sink in.

But you can do all this without PowerPoint.

Yes, you can.

So I don't have to use PowerPoint?

No, you don't. In fact, for many teachers in the Church, using a tool like PowerPoint or other presentation programs simply isn't a technological option. The bottom line is that there's a great benefit to using visual aids, but there are a lot of different ways to display images, from bringing in actual objects to showing pictures to using overheads to writing on the chalkboard. Of course, where you have the ability to use something like PowerPoint, it's very much worth considering.

Why? It looks so slick that it's got to be hard to use. And I feel like some people use it to cover up a lack of real analysis. I feel like their presentations become all style and no substance.

Those are a couple of the main concerns we often encounter with PowerPoint—that it's too hard to use and that it leads to slick rather than substantive presentations. Anything else? We may as well get all concerns on the table.

Okay, it also seems like it undermines the very thing you're pushing—student participation. Most of the time when I see people using PowerPoint, it just helps them illustrate their lecture. It's almost like they're wed to it. It seems like having an elaborate PowerPoint can get in the way of the kind of flexibility you'd need to really have a good discussion.

We'll start with the first objection—that the tool must be too hard to use. Interestingly enough, we hear this mostly from people who've never tried to learn how to use it. We both felt this way ourselves when we first saw PowerPoint: it looked so impressive that we figured it must be hard to learn. When so many other people are already experts in using the tool, it feels like the train has left the station without us. It leads some people to become some kind of retro-purists with the motto, "Long live the transparency!"

So what finally changed your mind?

Trying it. We were amazed that within thirty minutes we were able to put a basic presentation together.

Don't tell me that's all it took for you to master PowerPoint.

No, that's all it took for us to see just how easy it was to use it. Over time, we've learned a lot more bells and whistles, but after thirty minutes, we could create a simple presentation. We realized we'd been fools to let it scare us. In fact, whether talking about PowerPoint or any other teaching help that comes along, that's an important point: don't let the tool scare you. When Mark trains CES senior missionary couples going all over the world, he regularly tells them that when it comes to computers and technology, if they need help, they can just ask their students. If you're interested and patient, you can learn from the younger generation—and they are very willing to help. Imagine— a teacher learning from a student!

Some people don't have a laptop or a setup where they can show PowerPoint in their classrooms, so they obviously can't use it. But if you've got a tool like PowerPoint available and you refuse to use it because it's hard to learn, then your fear is robbing students of a potential benefit. In the end, it doesn't take much to learn how to use PowerPoint—and it's an effort worth making.

But even if you know how to use the tool, it seems like a lot of extra work to do for every lesson.

In some ways, it is. For us, investing time in preparing a slide show for our lessons makes more sense, since we can use those slide shows again the next time we teach the class. For the average Sunday School teacher, creating a PowerPoint for every lesson may not make sense. The fact is that you have only so much time to prepare each lesson. And if you're not careful, the creation of flashy slide shows can cut into the time needed to really craft the substance of the lesson— and you become a PowerPoint junkie. Make sure the tool doesn't end up controlling you (just like the Internet).

And yet, occasionally using slide shows with lessons can add a lot for those teachers who choose to do so. It simply takes discipline to make sure you're not taking time from the substance of your lesson preparation to create a stylish slide show. One way to do that is to prepare your lesson first. That way, you're never stealing time from your lesson preparation to prepare the slide show.

All right, but what about the lecturing problem? Even if you can use the tool efficiently, it still seems like it ends up making you follow your slides all the way through the lesson, with no room for discussion.

That may be the greatest challenge with using PowerPoint. To remain flexible and student-centered, you've got to be willing to do a couple of things: skip around in your slides and just not get to some of them.

Can you skip around in PowerPoint? I don't know that I've ever seen it done.

It's not difficult at all, really, but you do need to do two things: make a mental adjustment so that you're willing to skip around in your presentation, and then learn how to navigate through the program quickly. Once you do, it's easy enough to skip to slides throughout the program. But the urge to march sequentially through the slides and to lecture more is strong, so teachers who use PowerPoint have to be on their guard.

I'm still not sure I'm convinced about how much time this will take. If I understand you correctly, you're suggesting I don't steal any time from my lesson preparation to prepare slide shows. So isn't this really an add-on? Haven't I just increased my total lesson preparation time?

Maybe, at least if you weren't doing anything with visual aids before. But we can now create a slide show with a picture from the Gospel Art Picture Kit more quickly than we can find a hard copy of that same picture in the Gospel Art Picture Kit.[80] And we can create a slide with a quote on it more quickly than we can create an overhead with that same quote—and much more quickly than we can write it on the board. Plus we can add a picture of the prophet or apostle who made the statement, so our students become familiar with the Brethren.

There's no question that it may initially take you a bit longer to create slide shows. But it's an investment, kind of like learning to type. Once you progress a little up the learning curve, it becomes a very efficient way to do things. And as part of the investment, early on you'll probably spend some time gathering photographs of apostles and prophets or creating slide formats you like. But you only need to download the prophet's picture and pictures from the online Gospel Art Picture Kit once. After that, you can just cut and paste from slides you've already made. Basically, you spend time now to save time later.

One more question. I've seen some fancy musical slide shows. What do you think of those?

In light of what we've said about not letting the tool control you, you can't do these kinds of slide shows very often, but we have found that they can be powerful on special occasions. We love to put some pictures, some scripture quotes, and some General Authority quotes on a particular topic together with music; the combination can be pretty powerful. Our students routinely tell us about feeling the Spirit and being motivated to change in some way as a result of some of those kinds of presentations.

That doesn't sound like something I'd learn in the thirty-minute crash course.

It's probably not, although with help (remember to enlist your students or children!), you'd be surprised what you can put together pretty quickly.

Anything else?

Whether it's PowerPoint, transparencies, or pictures, we need to put in a plug for how helpful visual tools are to students who are visual learners. Since we have started using PowerPoint, we've been surprised how many students tell us that they learn much better when they can see things. We only regret that it took computers to help us see things from their point of view.

- Recognize that visual images in any medium can be very powerful tools.
- Don't let your fear of learning to use a new visual tool deprive your students of the benefits of that tool.
- As great as some visual tools are, never let the tool control your lesson or your lesson preparation.
- Remember that visual learners are very grateful when teachers find some way to illustrate principles rather than just talk about them.

FOURTEEN

THE RIGHT STUFF
AT THE RIGHT TIME

Teachers can have an extraordinary influence on students—if they have credibility with their students. Getting and keeping credibility includes not only living the gospel, as we've discussed in earlier chapters, but also getting our facts and quotes and doctrines right. However good our intentions, we build on a shaky foundation if we accidentally introduce some off-base doctrines along with the truths we teach. Keeping the doctrine in our classes pure also requires us to be aware of what we don't know—and to be willing to admit it.

Many of the students in my class know the gospel better than I do. What do I say when they ask a question and I don't know the answer? I feel like I should know the answer because I'm the teacher.

The sooner you learn to embrace the phrase *I don't really know,* the better off you'll be. Teachers who feel like they need to know all the answers end up giving some bad answers about things that either we don't know as a Church yet or they haven't really learned yet as individuals. We're much better off just saying that we don't know.

That sounds like a cop-out. Shouldn't I be studying and learning more so that I can answer all their questions?

Increasing our knowledge is good, and with the right kind of question we often promise to do a bit of research to see what answers we can find for the student. (Better yet, we like to point our students in the direction of some useful research tools like the Church's website and the scriptures so that they can look for answers themselves.) But if it's a deeper, more speculative question, like whether Heavenly Mother helped with the Creation, we might also say that we haven't read anything about it in the scriptures or heard anything about it in general conference talks, so while we can't rule it out as a possibility, it apparently isn't something the Lord feels we need to know.

The fact is there's plenty we don't know, even in the restored gospel of Jesus Christ. It's true that with modern revelation we have answers to many questions that the rest of the world doesn't. But sometimes that leads us to foolishly believe we have answers to *every* question. We don't. Teachers often get into doctrinal trouble when they feel compelled to come up with interpretations on matters where none have been given—at least by those whose interpretations matter. "Doctrinal interpretation is the province of the First Presidency," President Benson declared. "The Lord has given that stewardship to them by revelation. No teacher has the right to interpret doctrine for the members of the Church."[81]

Consider life after death, for example. With Doctrine and Covenants section 76, we have a far more detailed picture of post-mortal possibilities than the rest of the world has. And because we know much more about what happens when we die than those of other faiths or even other Christians do, we may sloppily assume that we know everything there is to know. But Joseph Smith himself said that if the people were ready and the Lord allowed him, he could "explain a hundredfold more" about the three degrees of glory than he previously had.[82] We like to use that quote to remind students about how much we still don't know. If our students can't come up with some questions about life after death to which we don't know the answer, they just need to be more inquisitive.

That's a very liberating attitude.

It is indeed. When we realize that it's no admission of defeat to confess we don't know the answer, it takes a lot of pressure off us.

That kind of attitude is not only liberating, it's also humble. Many teachers don't say, "I don't know" because they mistakenly think they *do* know the answer.

So how can I guard against doing that? If I'm pretty sure I know the answer to a particular question, why would I say I'm not sure?

One simple way to guard against accidentally teaching false doctrine is to check sources. The safest route is to answer questions and teach doctrines directly from the scriptures; then we know we're on sure ground. The next best thing is to read statements from approved lesson manuals and recent general conference talks. The Savior's commandment to Oliver Cowdery is particularly relevant for teachers: "I give unto you a commandment, that you rely upon the things which are written" (D&C 18:3). When we think about some of the questionable doctrine and wacky stuff we've heard in gospel classes over the years, it has almost never been something the teacher was actually reading. Instead, it was a quote the teacher was recalling from memory, or it was simply his or her own opinion about something. When students say, "Like the Savior said, 'I never said it would be easy—I only said it would be worth it,'" they obviously aren't reading from His word, because the Savior never said that in the scriptures.

What if students repeat quotes in class like that and we wonder about their accuracy?

That's a tough one, because teachers have to balance the need to ensure that correct doctrines are taught with the need to make sure students feel safe making comments in class. If we know the students are quoting something that's not accurate, we'll gently correct them: "The Brethren have, indeed, commented about how valiant the youth of the Church are today, but we actually need to set the record straight on the 'quote' you shared about today's youth having been generals in the war in heaven. . . ." And if the quote sounds questionable but doesn't clearly contradict well-established doctrines, we might say something like, "That's interesting—I've never heard that before. If you find that quote in writing, I'd love to see it." That leaves open the possibility that the quote is accurate but also lets students know that we're not endorsing it and have some question about its accuracy.

I've got one more question about speculative questions. What if you *do* know an answer to a very speculative question? There are some things I've learned from obscure quotes over the years that I don't hear preached a lot in general conference. If a student who's read *The Da Vinci Code* asks if Christ was married, do I share the quotes I've read on the subject?

First, the fact that decades ago a General Authority or two said something on a particular point does not establish that position as official Church doctrine. We need not feel obligated to disclose and defend every statement made on every topic by every Church leader of the past.[83]

Second, even if there is agreement on a particular historical detail or doctrinal position, we need to remember what we discussed in a previous chapter about timing. There's a time for every truth. And often, that time is not going to be in a Primary class or even a seminary or Gospel Doctrine class.

But isn't our job to teach the truth?

Yes, but not all the truth all the time. What if a Primary student asked a question about where babies come from? The teacher could diagram the entire reproductive process in class and teach nothing but truth. But Primary is hardly the time or place for sex education—even if it is taught accurately. Of course, that's an extreme example, but it underscores the fact that in deciding whether to teach something, we need to ask ourselves more than just whether it's true. We need to ask whether our class is the right time and right place to teach that doctrine or fact.

Okay, I can see how it would be inappropriate to teach about the reproductive process in Sunday School. But why would it ever be inappropriate to teach a true doctrine?

Paul taught the Corinthians with doctrinal milk because they weren't yet ready for the meat (see 1 Corinthians 3:2). And on some occasions, the Savior instructed His disciples not to tell others that He was the Christ or that He had performed a particular miracle.[84]

President Packer explained the importance of timing for gospel teachers this way:

> Some things that are true are not very useful. . . . Teaching some things that are true, prematurely or at the wrong time, can invite sorrow and heartbreak instead of the joy intended to accompany learning. . . . It matters very much not only *what* we are told but *when* we are told it. Be careful that you build faith rather than destroy it.[85]

The order of heaven seems to be to teach things "line upon line, precept upon precept" (2 Nephi 28:30), which runs counter to our natural tendency to dump everything we know about a subject on students who may not yet be ready.

How do you feel about teachers using stories?

Stories are great—they grab students' attention and can bring gospel principles to life. But wise teachers always use stories carefully. First, they make sure stories are the spice of the lesson, not the main course. Because students of all ages enjoy stories, it's tempting for teachers who are great storytellers to share story after story. Doing so is like feeding our children all ice cream and no vegetables. Second, wise teachers are careful to make gospel principles rather than themselves the stars of their stories. Finally, responsible teachers always make sure they get their stories right. Whether they are quotes or stories, when we get things wrong and students discover it later, we lose credibility in their eyes. They may even begin to doubt true principles that we taught along with stories that later proved to have been embellished or to simply have been myths.

As with quotes, a great way to avoid getting stories wrong is to verify their accuracy by tracking down a reliable written account. For example, we once heard a story about a mother bird who saved the lives of her chicks in the Yellowstone forest fires several years ago by tucking them under her wings. The mother died in the fire, sacrificing her life to save her chicks. It was a great story that would wonderfully augment the Savior's statements in 3 Nephi 10 about gathering Israel as a hen gathers her chickens. So we searched for the story on the Internet and found it on truthorfiction.com—along with a compelling explanation of why it is a myth.[86] The bottom line for us on this last point is that we rarely share a story unless we have a written account from a credible source or it happened to us personally.

Okay, this last question may seem odd, but it's genuine. What about doubt? I've seen different teachers handle their own doubts quite differently—including some being very public about their doubts and even their criticisms of Church leaders.

It's one thing to privately wonder about a doctrine or even publicly admit that we don't fully understand exactly how to explain something like Rebekah and Jacob's conduct in procuring a blessing for Jacob from Isaac (see Genesis 27). But it's quite another to sow seeds of doubt as a gospel teacher. It may be our constitutional right as citizens to doubt and criticize, but it's our covenantal duty as Saints to build faith rather than tear it down.

Most teachers are honest enough to ask to be released if they can no longer in good faith teach the doctrines they have been called, appointed, or hired to teach. But there are a few who, doctrinally speaking, are like the parents Elder Jeffrey R. Holland described who, "always like to pitch their tents out on the periphery of religious faith." Elder Holland's counsel to such parents applies with almost equal force to teachers:

> In this Church there is an enormous amount of room—and scriptural commandment—for studying and learning, for comparing and considering, for discussion and awaiting further revelation. . . . In this there is no place for coercion or manipulation, no place for intimidation or hypocrisy. But no child in this Church should be left with uncertainty about his or her parents' devotion to the Lord Jesus Christ, the Restoration of His Church, and the reality of living prophets and apostles. . . . In such basic matters of

faith, prophets do not apologize for requesting unity, indeed conformity, in the eloquent sense that the Prophet Joseph Smith used that latter word (see D&C 128:13). . . .

[Teachers] simply cannot flirt with skepticism or cynicism, then be surprised when their [students] expand that flirtation into full-blown romance. . . . No, we can hardly expect the [students] to get to shore safely if the [teachers] don't seem to know where to anchor their own boat.[87]

Elder Bruce R. McConkie summarized a teacher's role in this way: "Agents represent their principal. They have no power of their own. They act in someone else's name. They do what they are told to do. They say what they are authorized to say—nothing more, nothing less."[88] In sum, gospel teachers have to remember that they are agents of a divine Principal—the Master Teacher—not independent contractors.

- Learn to say, "I don't know."
- There are plenty of doctrinal questions to which we don't actually know the answers.
- Rely on written sources to ensure the accuracy of the statements and stories you share.
- It's not enough to teach the truth; gospel teachers should teach the right doctrines at the right times.
- Stories can add variety to lessons—if they are accurate and promote doctrines rather than the story-tellers.
- As agents of the Lord, gospel teachers should never do anything to undermine the faith of their students.

FIFTEEN
NO WHIPPING THE STUDENTS

For many teachers of youth and children, one of the greatest challenges is maintaining some kind of order in the classroom without, say, whipping the students (something discouraged in most wards). Although we have no magic bullets for unruly classes, we find that most discipline problems can be avoided or managed well if we pay attention to a few key principles: building rapport, distracting students as needed, playing good offense, escalating responses gradually, and allowing students to save face.

What can I do to avoid becoming the uptight librarian, the perpetual shusher? I'm just not very patient with disruptive students, but I feel that I'm not very effective as a teacher when I get in that mode.

It's true that the more annoyed we become, the less we have the Spirit with us and the harder it is for us to teach. Once you become the shusher—especially an irritated shusher—students sense your irritability, like sharks smelling blood. Then it starts to turn into a battle, like Mark's eighth-grade English class with Ms. Penrose. Mark stopped listening to what she was saying and started looking for ways to annoy her. (He deserves every overactive student he's ever taught!) When teachers get in the uptight librarian mode, even if they win the battle and finally impose silence, they may well lose the war. Students will simply shut down—they may close their mouths, but they'll also close their minds and hearts.

So how do I avoid getting into that mode? It would be great if my students always behaved, but they don't. If I don't shush them, the class becomes chaotic.

We're not saying teachers should never shush their students. But the wise use of the tools we discuss here can help us not have to beg our classes to be quiet. Just as a wise parent slowly increases consequences for poor behavior, there are things gospel teachers can do to help control the classroom atmosphere rather than constantly shushing. And the first step in doing that is building rapport with students. The better relationship teachers have with their students, the less of an issue discipline becomes. That's one of many reasons it pays to spend a bit of time before class trying to get to know your students. As they sense you care about them, they respond much more quickly to your requests for them to settle down.

Of course, there is a difference between building good relationships with students and trying to be their buddies. Good teachers understand that they need to establish and enforce certain rules of classroom conduct. But they don't get more excited about those rules than they do about their lessons. If students feel like a teacher is throwing down the gauntlet, they'll rise to the challenge—and soon the teacher will have a full-fledged power struggle to deal with. Building rapport with students helps both students and teachers remember that they're on the same team, not battling each other for control of the classroom.

So how do you build rapport with teenagers or children? That just doesn't come naturally to me.

One key is to come to class prepared and early, so that you can spend those critical minutes before class talking with students as they arrive rather than scrambling to get things ready. Start by learning their names—whether you're teaching Primary, Gospel Doctrine, seminary, or institute. The sooner you know each student and can call on him or her by name, the sooner you can really begin to connect with them. (Some of Rob's colleagues at BYU—Idaho convinced him of the importance of this even in a college setting, so every semester he tries to follow their example and learn the names of nearly 300 students.)

As you begin to get to know them, ask them simple questions about their lives. How did their basketball game go? How do they like their new job? What did they get for their birthday? Joke with them and interact with them as a real person. "Great teachers not only know the subject they are teaching but, just as important, they understand the needs of their students," Elder Hales noted. That's why, he suggests, we should "get to know what is happening in the lives of [our students]."[89]

In fact, especially for those working in the Young Men and Young Women organizations, seeing students outside of class not only improves teaching moments in the classroom, but it also creates teaching moments outside the classroom. And President Hunter taught that those extracurricular opportunities may be some of the best teaching moments: "Remember that the very best teaching is one on one and often takes place out of the classroom."[90]

Won't students know if you're just faking your interest in them?

Yes—so don't. Make sure your interest is genuine. For example, serving in the Young Men organization, we have always found that the time we spend with youth *out of class* on Tuesday or Wednesday helps us connect with them more powerfully *in class* on Sunday. So at Mutual each week we make a conscious effort to focus on getting to know the youth and interacting with them rather than merely chatting with other adult leaders. And when our schedules have permitted, we find we earn a lot of good will with students by showing up to support them at their games or performances. Even when Mark was in graduate school and an elders quorum president, he still found time to meet a couple of rather rowdy sophomore boys to play basketball after school with another teacher. It made a big difference in the boys' behavior in class and "put money in the bank" for when he occasionally had to ask them to be quiet.

The benefits of truly getting to know students go beyond just making the students more likely to settle down for a teacher they have come to appreciate. Rob remembers teaching a seminary student who seemed to have more than his share of attitude; at times, it felt like they were engaged in a bit of a power struggle. Then one day a wonderful young woman from a different period of seminary stopped by before class and asked if she could leave some cookies for him. "Is it his birthday?" Rob asked.

"No," this spiritually astute young woman explained, "it's his sister. I don't know what the disease is that she has, but she's been slowly dying, and it's getting near the end. It's been pretty hard on their family." Rob felt terrible when he realized that this young man had had more than enough reason to be a bit out of sorts. As he was filled with compassion (and some guilt), Rob's attitude toward the young man changed completely—and so did their teacher–student relationship. Discipline problems pretty much disappeared as Rob became filled with the genuine concern he should have felt all along for this student.

As you truly get to know your students, you will better know how to handle them. Instead of viewing Jeff as a hyper kid who's out of control, you'll know him well enough to view him as a kid who is amazingly kind to his sister and is remarkably active in the Church, despite coming from a semiactive home—and as a kid who just happens to have a lot of energy. Knowing that Ashley's parents are going through a divorce will give you much more patience with her in class when she acts out so people will pay attention to her. The more we understand our students, the more we love them and the less we tend to be annoyed by their quirks. And when we're less irritated and more full of love, we're much more effective at getting order in the classroom.

But surely knowing students well and having a good rapport with them doesn't eliminate all your discipline problems. I know that sometimes as a student I've probably talked with friends too much during class, even when I knew and liked the teacher.

Building rapport with students provides a great foundation for dealing with disciplinary problems, but other tools are definitely needed. One of the first things we use when a class is getting out of hand is what we call distraction. The idea is simple. Rather than repeatedly asking for people to be quiet, simply change to a different activity that might grab their attention. In a way, opening hymns and prayers do that quite effectively in most of our meetings; they signal to us that the time has come to stop talking with our friends and to turn our attention to the front of the room.

I'm not sure I follow. What kind of things can I do to redirect students' attention?

When one of our children is crying, asking them to stop usually isn't too effective—and demanding that they stop pretty much backfires completely. But when we shift their focus by asking questions like, "What's the first thing you're going to do when you get to Disneyland next month?" it's easier for them to move forward. The principle is basically the same with students in a class. We often see more success in getting them to be quiet by giving them something different to focus on than by simply asking them to be quiet. It doesn't always work, but if you've got another activity—especially one that will force them to be quiet, like searching in their scriptures, or one that will grab their attention, like a video clip or object lesson or a great personal story—then moving to that activity quickly can be a good way to restore order.

Let's say you've had a great beginning to the class, but somehow it's degenerated into all of the students talking with their neighbors about their favorite scar stories. (This really happened, as a matter of fact.) Your next step in the lesson is a video, which you'd planned to set up with a few remarks. You nicely ask the kids to give you their attention, but it has almost no effect. So you simply turn out the lights and start the video. It's amazing how quickly they'll get quiet.

But if you do that, you don't get to set up the video like you planned.

You can always do it quickly at the start of the video. Or hit the pause button 30 seconds into it and then set it up. And even if you couldn't set it up at all, it might be a good trade. You give up a little something you'd hoped to say, but in exchange you get their attention, without shushing them once.

But what if I'd really rather just shush them?

We do shush our students—probably more than we should. But we try to fight the urge. Whenever we feel the urge to tell everybody to be quiet *right now,* we try to ask ourselves, "Is there some way I could distract them into silence by changing activities or redirecting their attention?" Sometimes it's simply a matter of giving them an urgent task, such as telling them they have 60 seconds to count how many times the word *remember* is used in Helaman 5. The shift can even be emphasized by counting a brief countdown—three, two, one—and then starting a stopwatch. Mark uses this technique frequently with good results, and it has now become the standard method in Rob's family for getting people to be quiet for family prayer. In fact, whenever Rob's youngest child is ready for people to stop talking and get on with family prayer or mealtime prayer, he simply shouts out, "Three, two, one!" and bows his head.

I've noticed that some of the best teachers don't really seem to have as many discipline problems, while those who struggle with their lessons also happen to have the added challenge of unruly students. It's almost unfair.

That may seem unfair, but it's not. It's a simple matter of cause and effect.

What do you mean?

Boring lessons bring out the unruliness in students. Just as it's easier to get students to be quiet by switching to an interesting activity than by asking them to be quiet, generally the best defense against discipline problems is a good offense. In our experience of observing teachers of youth, there is almost a direct correlation between discipline problems and the quality of the lessons. The more boring and less engaging the lesson, the more likely the kids are to become restless and rowdy. Elder Boyd K. Packer put it this way: "As long as you are feeding the students well, few discipline problems will occur."[91] So if you find you're having lots of discipline problems, one of the wisest things you can do to improve the situation is prayerfully ponder ways to improve the quality of your lessons.

Fair enough. But even the most interesting teachers sometimes have to do more than build rapport, distract students, and teach great lessons. Do you ever kick kids out of class?

Yes, but rarely. Before teachers get to that nuclear option, they should have exhausted not just their patience, but a variety of other options first. Good parents and good international leaders do the same thing: they deal with problems rather than ignore them, but they escalate their responses gradually rather than overreact out of anger. They start with the most diplomatic response and work their way up from there. No bombing people just because you discovered they had a spy working in your embassy. And no kicking kids out of class just because they were talking too much. As President Packer puts it, "Most situations can be controlled with even a slight gesture," but some teachers "foolishly use the heavy artillery when small-arms fire would have won the battle."[92]

Sometimes in relationships—both personal and international—we find ourselves suddenly exploding because we've become fed up with someone else's conduct. Such outbursts are less likely to occur if we have productively and calmly addressed issues as they've arisen. The same is true for teachers. None of the things we've set forth here should be construed to mean that teachers should ignore disciplinary problems. First, try to avoid them by building good relationships with students and providing great lessons. Then try to get students back on track by switching activities quickly to regain their focus. But when those techniques don't work and students are disruptive, deal with those disruptions as they occur rather than holding your frustration inside until you finally explode in anger at your students.

How? What are some things you can do, then, in between distracting students and kicking them out?

Start with simple things, like saying, "That was a great comment, Quinn." Then turn to the part of the class that's making the most noise and ask, "Did you guys hear that? Quinn, say that one more time. I want everybody to hear it." Or call on those who've been creating a disturbance to read the next verse aloud. That forces them to stop their conversation, and it often sends the message—in a very polite way—that you've noticed them talking and would like them to stop.

You must have very good kids if that's all you need to do.

We do—and so do you. They're not that different than us when it comes to wanting to talk with their friends. Frankly, the two of us sometimes had to make sure we didn't sit next to each other during in-service meetings because we knew we'd end up talking or whispering too much and distracting each other. When we remember that, it's easier to give our students easy opportunities to get back in line, and most of them will. If we start bombing too quickly, we may do more harm than good.

What other tools do you use when those subtler approaches don't work?

Other time-tested techniques include standing closer to the students who are being too loud or occasionally making eye contact with them, which is sometimes enough if you have good rapport. And humor is one of the best ways to diffuse a lot of situations. Sometimes you can get away with a lot if you do it with a smile or a joke. Keep your requests polite, low-key, or even funny for as long as you can. Don't get heavy on them unless those kinds of attempts fail.

What if you've got a couple of kids who just keep talking to each other? They might be quiet for a while when you do one of these lower level things, but in the end, they stray into sidebar conversations.

With a youth class, we move them.

You mean you use a seating chart? That seems so old-school.

When Rob first started teaching, it seemed old-fashioned and unnecessary to him too. But one of the first things he observed when watching Mark was that he had a specific seat for each student. When quizzed about this, Mark confessed that even though he'd been teaching for over fifteen years, he still instituted a seating chart on the first or second day of class. A seating chart does wonders in breaking up chatty friends and building fortresses of quiet people around our most talkative students. A class that just won't be quiet without a seating chart can become entirely manageable almost overnight by using one.

But once you've got them in place, isn't it kind of offensive to them if you tell a couple of them they've got to move?

It can be, which is why it's not the first step to take in dealing with talkative friends. First, try more subtle things, even jokingly warning them by saying something like, "Don't make me move you. . . ." But if you do end up needing to move them, you can still knock off the rough edges.

How?

If it's been a while since you've changed the seating chart, you can just mix up the whole class. That way, no one feels singled out. Or if you need to move just a couple of people, you can smile and say, "You two looked like you were having way too much fun together. We can't have that!" And when they complain, you can tell them that you'd also be prone to talk with your best friend if you were sitting next to him or her.

The idea is not to make them feel bad unnecessarily. Whenever you're disciplining students, it's important to give them a way to save face. Give them an out so they don't look bad in front of their friends. When a teacher challenges a student unnecessarily in front of the class, the student will feel like cornered and defensive. It's important to keep order, but it's also important to do it in a way that lets students save face and feel respected.

This all sounds well and good, but I've been in classes where teachers were so worried about being students' friends that they imposed no discipline at all, and the class was sheer chaos.

Both of us have had to confront kids directly and, on rare occasions, have even had to ask someone to leave the class. It's just that you can address most discipline problems a lot better if you've got a good relationship with the students, if you try distraction before confrontation, and if you work your way up gradually instead of quickly taking more severe measures. And you won't have as many discipline problems to deal with if you're preparing well and feeding the students spiritually.

But we're definitely not saying to let the students do whatever they want. Good teachers have to be committed to keeping order in the classroom. Teachers who aren't willing to do anything to maintain discipline in the classroom often have the students run roughshod over them. But we are saying that the best way to keep them with you is by using subtle, Christlike methods rather than being heavy-handed right out of the gate.

What do you do with students who just don't respond to your more diplomatic methods?

Remember, don't give up the fight to keep order in the classroom just because your diplomatic efforts have failed. If the students are still misbehaving, ratchet up what you do. You might pull a student aside and talk to him or her individually about how his or her behavior is affecting the rest of the class. And on very rare occasions, after working with parents and priesthood leaders, you may actually have to ask students not to attend your class if they're not willing to play by the rules. Most of them will agree to obey the rules. Only once in his twenty years with CES has Mark had a student who decided to stop coming after that kind of conversation. And while Mark regretted that this boy chose not to come anymore, when the student left, it changed the whole tenor of the class. His leaving saved seminary that year for the rest of those students. President David O. McKay counseled teachers about severe disciplinary actions this way: "Any teacher can dismiss a boy; you should exhaust all your other sources before you come to that. But order we *must* have! . . . Better one boy starve than an entire class be slowly poisoned."[93]

Finally, remember that there's a balance between maintaining order so that students can feel the Spirit and actually driving out the Spirit by becoming obsessed with discipline. Sometimes, the antics of one or two students can make it difficult for a whole class to feel the Spirit. Teachers who fail to address those kinds of problems do so at the expense of the class as a whole. Lasting change won't occur in students if a teacher decides just to be a "facilitating friend" and lets students run wild.

On the other hand, order itself is not the ultimate goal. The ultimate goal is to provide an atmosphere where the Spirit thrives and where lives are changed. We've seen teachers who act as if maintaining good discipline is the highest priority. And they definitely succeed in achieving that aim. But they rarely succeed in the real goal of changing students' lives, because the students aren't really engaged. The students simply refuse to open up and participate, so no real change takes place.

Great teachers manage to maintain discipline without injuring relationships. They truly care about their students, and their love is evident in the way they try to establish discipline. In the end, by following the kinds of principles described in this chapter, successful teachers strike the balance required to maintain good relationships and good discipline at the same time.

- When possible, avoid shushing battles with students.
- Build rapport with students by genuinely caring about their lives.
- When students become restless, refocus their attention by shifting gears to a different type of activity.
- Know that the best defense against disciplinary problems is a good offense—a great lesson.
- Escalate disciplinary action gradually.
- Remember that order is not your only goal, or you may end up with students who close their hearts along with their mouths.

SIXTEEN

MANAGING THE CLOCK

In a sport with a clock, great athletes who lead their teams have an exceptional awareness of the time left in the game. They are not unduly rushed, but they are also never surprised when the clock suddenly expires with their team far from where they need to be on the field or court. Knowing how much time remains and roughly how much time it takes to do certain things, these champions know just how to pace themselves.

In much the same way, great teachers are masters of the clock. They know exactly when their class ends, they know how much time they have left, and they know roughly how much they can cover in that period of time. And like a good quarterback, there's nothing passive about great teachers as they manage class time. They let class members know when they only want rapid fire comments, they end some discussions and move on to others, and they may drop out entire portions of some of the material they had planned to cover.

I admit it: I pretty much just teach until I'm done covering the material I've prepared. What's wrong with that?

Nothing—if you're lucky enough to end right on time. But most people who have prepared thoroughly or allow some discussion will end up with more material to cover than there are minutes in a class. That means that one of three things will happen: (1) class runs long, (2) the teacher tries to cover twenty minutes of material in the last five minutes, or (3) the teacher simply leaves out the last quarter or third or half of his lesson.

At the risk of stating the obvious, let us point out why none of these is good. In the first scenario, most students squirm in their seats and don't catch a word of what the teacher is saying. And teachers who consistently run over their allotted time may breed resentment, since their conduct suggests they believe that whatever they have to say is more important than whatever else students may have planned or needed to do. When teaching seminary or college classes, for example, we may make our students late for their next class. When running over in a Sunday class, we may cut into the lesson time of the teacher who follows us, or we may delay a whole family's ability to go home for dinner because they are waiting for one of our students. Mark was in a ward where fast and testimony meeting consistently went ten to twenty minutes overtime. Within a month of being put in the bishopric, Mark was asked independently by four or five members if something couldn't be done to curtail this problem. When we end class punctually, we show respect for our students. And if we insist on beginning class on time and expect our students to arrive on time, we are also being consistent.

The second and third scenarios are virtually synonymous, since students usually get almost nothing out of hyperspeed summaries. The problem with either approach is that the chronology of the material, rather than the importance of the material, determines what gets left out. The last principle we plan to cover in our lesson plan may be the most important principle of the day, but our students don't get to hear it if we run out of time.

Perhaps the most important thing in managing the clock is making conscious, inspired choices about what to leave out—rather than leaving it to the clock. Teachers who don't proactively ration the time in their lesson almost always end up having to skip something, sail through it, or run overtime—and it may be the most important concept that gets left out.

That's why it's very helpful for teachers, especially when they're just getting started, to estimate how much time they want to spend on each portion of their lesson. That first step alone often shows teachers that they've got far more in their lesson plan than they can realistically cover. Once Rob has scaled back the lesson and has come up with realistic estimates for how long each part will take, one technique he occasionally uses is writing the expected time of arrival for a couple of key points in the lesson. He finds that writing the actual time (say, 2:25 PM) instead of just the minutes each section will take saves him the trouble of trying to do any math in his head during the lesson. At 2:25, he can then see exactly where he is compared to where he had planned to be at the midpoint of his lesson.

But if you've got your lesson well prepared in advance, doesn't the timing kind of take care of itself?

For experienced teachers who've practiced pacing themselves and rationing their time, it might. But not for most teachers.

Most of the time when teachers squeeze twenty minutes of material into the last five minutes, they don't realize their predicament until the last five minutes of class. They most likely haven't even thought through just how long they expected their lesson would take. Instead, they've simply prepared a lesson with all the thoughts they've got pertaining to the subject of the lesson—without taking the vital step of sizing up the lesson plan and estimating how long it will take.

But it's so hard to predict.

True, but many teachers and speakers never even try. Even when you take this step, you'll still have to be flexible and make adjustments on the fly. But if you do your best job of estimating in advance how long each part of your lesson will take, you can often do some valuable pruning of the lesson plan up front by realizing that there's simply too much material to cover in the allotted time.

You can tell when this kind of adjustment hasn't happened, for example, when the last speaker in sacrament meeting reads his talk and runs long by ten minutes. The speaker knows—or should know—his talk will take twenty minutes to read and that there are only ten minutes left in the meeting when he starts to speak, but he forges ahead and reads his talk without cutting out anything.

But it's not his fault if the speakers before him ran long.

It's true that each speaker has a responsibility to stay within his or her allotted time. But for the reasons we mentioned earlier about ending class on time, it's especially important that the last speaker end on time. Consciously choosing to run over—unless you're the presiding authority—is disrespectful to all those teachers in the ward who have spent so much time preparing lessons that they will now have to cut short.

But what if it's not so much a conscious decision? What if the speaker is simply giving the talk he prepared without realizing he'll run over?

That's just our point: the result is the same. So speakers need to be aware of when they are going to run over and need to cut something from their talk. And they can do that much better if they have taken the preparatory step of determining in advance how long their lesson or talk will take. In the case of speakers who read their talks, there's no real excuse for not knowing how long their talk will take if it is read at a normal speed.

Consciously planning ahead to manage the clock not only saves teachers and speakers (and those who listen to them) a lot of grief, but it also allows them to spend the most time on the most important principles. For example, imagine visiting a Gospel Doctrine class on Jacob 5, Zenos's allegory. There are a lot of different points you could try to draw out of that allegory, but two of the most important points would certainly be the Savior's love for us and His continual efforts on our behalf, as well as the great need for more laborers to help in the last days.

The teacher who valiantly attempts to take the class through each step of grafting and pruning will almost certainly run out of time to discuss the principles from the allegory that can make a difference in students' lives. Rob once visited a class where this very thing happened. The teacher didn't even make it halfway through the chapter before time ran out. About five minutes into the lesson, it was clear to Rob that there was no way the class was going to get to the point of the story. The teacher was spending so much time examining each tree that she didn't have time to step back and see the patterns in the forest.

So skip ahead to the principles being taught?

Not exactly. Detailed scriptural analysis is actually where we want to spend our time. In fact, sometimes we might spend a whole lesson putting a couple of verses under what we call the "Scripture Microscope," where we dig into each word and phrase. Our concern is when teachers do that inadvertently, leaving themselves no time to get to the most important points because they were methodically plowing through each verse. That's probably what happened in the class Rob observed.

When did the teacher realize her predicament?

About five minutes before the class was over, and by that time it was too late. Mark has seen the same thing happen dozens of times in observing young full-time and early-morning seminary teachers. After the lesson they'll say, "I didn't even get to the best part of my lesson. I wish I'd had more time."

Okay, I admit I've been that teacher before. I can see that trying to chart out a schedule for a lesson would help. But in this book you've been hammering home the importance of participation. It seems to me that participation throws a huge wrench into the works. It's such a big variable, since you never know how much a class will participate.

That's true. It's much easier to know how long it will take to read a presentation than how long it will take to cover material with plenty of student participation. Generally, as we mentioned in discussing student involvement, you can't cover as much material with a good class that involves participation as you can in a lecture. So you need to be sure to trim the breadth of your subject matter enough to allow for some depth in discussion.

But I've seen Gospel Doctrine discussions that never seem to end. It's almost as if you could spend the whole lesson on a single verse.

That's why great teachers actively guide the discussion rather than passively let it wander along its course.

What do you mean?

Just because we want participation doesn't mean the teacher needs to let the class completely dictate the flow of the lesson. It's perfectly appropriate to allot a certain amount of time for the discussion of a particular principle and then move on, even if the class would like to discuss it for another twenty minutes.

None of the counsel calling for greater student participation requires teachers to give up control of the classroom. On the contrary, while teachers who orchestrate discussion rather than merely lecture will often allow some improvised deviation, they must actively conduct and guide the conversation to keep it productive and relevant. In fact, it's your duty to move things along at times, unless you feel inspired to spend the whole lesson on the topic at hand. You know what's coming in the rest of the lesson and what will get skipped if the discussion of one point goes on too long. The class doesn't know, or at least they're not focused on it. So it's your job to help push ahead to make sure you can get to other important principles.

How do you do that? I can't quite see saying, "I'm sorry, Brother Jones, but you need to be quiet now so I can move on with the lesson."

We do try to avoid telling people to clam up. But you can do a lot with some simple, subtle phrases. If we want several short comments on a subject instead of lengthier personal insights, we might introduce the question by saying, "Let's quickly list some of the adjectives describing a good missionary that appear in Alma 38. Just rattle some off, but only one apiece. Go." That sends a message that you're looking for short phrases, not paragraphs, from students. Then if you want to build on any answer, you can always stop and ask a follow-up question, like, "What do you think it means to be bold but not overbearing?"

Another simple technique we'll use when we want to move things along is to limit additional comments by throwing out a number and telling the class why. We might say, "These are great comments, but we need to move on to Alma's conversation with Shiblon, so let me just take three more comments." That lets class members know where we're going and helps them regulate their input just a bit. We figure that there's no need to keep the class in the dark about how we want to allot the lesson time. If they know we want to spend the final fifteen minutes of class on the last chapter of the Sermon on the Mount, they can sometimes help manage the discussion.

Even then, some folks have a hard time stifling themselves. They're just desperate to add their two cents' worth, even though we've called on the last three people. Sometimes we'll stretch a bit and take one more answer, but often we'll wrap up the discussion of a section by saying something like, "We could spend the whole lesson discussing Alma 38 because it's so full of insights into qualities great missionaries have, but we really need to spend some time talking about what Alma teaches his son who wasn't such a great missionary."

That reminds me of the problem of the Big Talkers. Their comments may be great, but they tend to dominate the class discussion, squeezing other class members out of the discussion without knowing it. Is there any way to rein them in?

One thing we try at the outset of each semester is to have a discussion about the importance of participation. As part of that discussion, we'll acknowledge that a few folks, like us, would like to answer every question, while some people, like Rob's wife, would be happy never to participate. Because we believe everyone has useful insights to share, we explain, our goal is to have as many people as possible participate. That means some people (like Rob's wife) need to stretch themselves and take some risks. But it also means that other people (like us) may need to limit the number of comments we make so that there's time for others to comment as well. In fact, we explain that we're tempted to raise our hand in response to every question in Gospel Doctrine, but over the years we've learned to try to regulate ourselves and choose just two or three comments so that others will have a chance. By noting that we struggle with this and telling others how we handle it, we make it acceptable for Big Talkers to acknowledge this tendency in themselves. It's not a fatal character flaw, just something to keep in check—out of consideration for others.

As part of that initial discussion, it's helpful to forewarn people that you may not always call on them when they raise their hand. "Don't be offended if you're a frequent commenter and I don't immediately call on you when you raise your hand," Rob tells his students at the outset of each semester. "I might be trying to give someone else a chance to participate."

It's important to follow through on that throughout the year, sometimes giving subtle reminders: "Let's hear from someone who hasn't had a chance to comment yet." Or if the problem persists, you might even be more explicit: "How many of you have not made a comment yet today? Before we hear more comments from those who've already had a chance, I'd like to hear from some of you."

A few times when Big Talkers become a chronic problem in a class, we've announced at the beginning of class that we want to see how many different people we can get to comment that day. We even ask a student to track the number and periodically check on our progress as a class. "What are we up to now? Seven? Let's hear from some of the rest of you." That sends a message to the people who haven't participated yet that we really want their participation, while simultaneously suggesting to the Big Talkers that they rein themselves in.

Usually these subtle techniques are enough to do the job, but occasionally you may encounter students who are Huge Talkers. And they don't pick up on hints, even as the hints become increasingly less subtle. In this case, try pulling them aside after class and being up front about the challenge.

Rob once had a Huge Talker who had no idea how annoyed the other students were getting with him. So Rob took him aside after class and reminded him about the class goal of getting as many people as possible to participate. Rob asked how he thought that was going and what the class could do to improve in terms of having a lot of people participate. The boy finally came to the conclusion that maybe he needed to make fewer comments. He had a great heart, but he was just kind of socially unaware, so Rob told him about how he limits himself to two or three comments in Gospel Doctrine and suggested he do the same. For the next couple of days, when he raised his hand for the fourth time, looking like he'd burst if Rob didn't call on him, Rob actually held up three fingers to remind him of their conversation. After that, he finally got the message and did a much better job of reining himself in.

Let's go back to the other end of the spectrum, since I'm still much more worried about no participation than too much participation. What if I've trimmed and pruned my lesson in hopes of all this participation, and then the students participate about as much as a bump on a log? Now I'm stuck with this scaled back lesson and ten minutes left at the end of class.

Build in accordion sections.

What are those?

They're sections that you can expand or shrink or delete as necessary, usually about a principle that's worth discussing but can be thrown overboard if necessary. It's like what a wise stake president does at stake conference, especially if he's got a visiting General Authority. Like your lesson, he's got the speakers scheduled to end at certain times so that there will be plenty of time for the presiding authority's concluding remarks. But he knows that some speakers might run over their times, leaving the presiding authority less time to speak. To compensate for this problem, some stake presidents schedule a speaker toward the end of the meeting whose job is to shorten his talk as necessary to get the meeting back on track. That speaker provides built-in flexibility.

An accordion section does just that for a good teacher. About half or two thirds of the way through your lesson plan, include a section on a principle that's worth discussing but would be the one subpoint or principle you would want to drop from the lesson if there were not enough time to cover everything. If you're on track in terms of time when you get to that point in your lesson, then you explore the accordion section fully with plenty of discussion. But if there's not as much time, you cover it briefly without opening things up for discussion. And if there's no time, you drop it from the lesson altogether—and you've just bought yourself ten minutes. It gives you a way to get back on track without just rushing through material.

Any final thoughts?

In a book, it's easy to get the final word. In a class, it can be more difficult. That's why it's important to save time for a conclusion. Once you get the students in the habit of participating, they'll often make comments right up until the closing prayer.

Is that a problem? I thought that's what I was shooting for.

It's not terrible by any means, and sometimes we'll let that happen. But as a rule, we think there are some real benefits to taking at least one or two minutes at the end of the lesson and tying things together, often with a closing testimony. It's just one more quick repetition of the key principles of the lesson that can help inscribe the lesson's messages on students' hearts. A great conclusion includes ending the lesson on a strong note with a testimony that ties together the themes the teacher has woven throughout the lesson. But you only get time for that final shot if you successfully manage the clock.

- Manage the clock so you can make conscious choices about what to leave out—rather than just racing through or skipping important material at the end of the lesson.
- Estimate how long portions of your lesson will take so you can better pace yourself.
- Actively guide discussions rather than let them wander endlessly.
- Don't let a few Big Talkers dominate the discussion.
- Use accordion sections to create flexibility.
- Save some time for a conclusion.

SEVENTEEN
Fun and "Fried Froth"

We once asked a young early-morning seminary teacher how he enjoyed teaching. "It's easy," he said with a smile. "I've got a list of games, and I just keep a couple to play every day. That keeps them happy."

It's easy for an aunt or uncle to become popular with visiting children: just let them eat whatever they want. But good parents are concerned more about their children's long-term health and happiness than they are about their own short-term popularity—so they feed their children vegetables even when the children would rather have ice cream.

Great teachers are the same way. They're more concerned about what students will think of them in ten years than in ten minutes.

I want to be liked in ten minutes *and* in ten years.

Most teachers who will be liked by their students ten years from now will be liked by their students ten minutes from now. But if we have to choose between the two, we'd rather be appreciated in the long run than liked in the short run.

So as a practical matter, how does that change the way you teach?

It means we aim to edify rather than entertain our students. It means we tell them what they need to hear, not necessarily what they want to hear.

Providing needed counsel rather than just pleasing praise is just as important and difficult for leaders in employment situations. For example, Mark has had eight area directors supervise him throughout his career with CES. Among other duties, an area director observes each teacher in his geographical area a minimum of once a year. During these observations Mark has most often received feedback such as, "Just keep doing what you're doing," or "Your class was really good today." One even said, "I've got no room to give you any input. I couldn't do the daily grind of seminary." That was always very nice to hear. But as previously mentioned in this book, the one area director that gave him specific feedback on things he could change really made a difference and helped him improve as a teacher.

Rob worked for a few years as an executive, and he found that there were many consultants eager to tell him what he wanted to hear. After all, they were eager to maintain good relations and keep a lucrative business contract. In the short term, then, there was some pressure for them to say whatever would keep their client happy. But over the long term, Rob always appreciated most those consultants who had the courage to tell him what he needed to hear, not just what he wanted to hear.

With gospel teachers, too, there's a strong pull to keep the students happy, whether it's by playing games, cutting class short, or just telling entertaining stories. But years later—whether in this life or the next—those same students who begged you to play hangman will wish you'd never given in. In short, gospel teachers in particular must beware of the temptation to become popular.

I don't think I'll have to worry about that. I know I'll never be their favorite teacher. I'm just hoping they don't run me out of the class.

The temptation to care too much about whether students like you isn't an issue just for dynamic, popular teachers. Even the most boring and unpopular teachers (which won't be you, by the way) can be tempted to alter their lesson plan to get students to like them more. It's surprising how much pressure a teacher can feel from a class of teenagers. It's not that you want to be the most popular teacher or have a following or anything. But when you hear other classes having great fun playing games all the time and your students beg you to play more games, it's really tempting to give them what they want. Similarly, Rob noticed that when he raised the bar and started requiring more of his BYU—Idaho students in the syllabus, more students began dropping his classes at the beginning of the semester. Even though he felt strongly that he was doing the right thing, he still felt a pull—which he resisted—to water down his classes so that students wouldn't drop them.

Whatever the particulars, when we dilute the gospel so that students will like us, we're guilty of a form of priestcraft. When we shortchange the scriptures and doctrine to fill our classes with stories so that students will like us more—when it's more important to us that our students laugh than that they understand the doctrine—then we've crossed the line.

It's a natural temptation. In fact, Elder Dallin H. Oaks has said that the most popular teachers "have a special susceptibility to priestcraft":

> With a trained mind and a skillful manner of presentation, teachers can become unusually popular and effective in teaching. But Satan will try to use that strength to corrupt teachers by encouraging them to gather a following of disciples. A Church teacher, Church Education System instructor, or Latter-day Saint university professor who gathers such a following and does this "for the sake of riches and honor" (Alma 1:16) is guilty of priestcraft.[94]

Elder Paul V. Johnson, who is also the CES administrator of religious education, calls priestcraft "an occupational hazard," at least for full-time teachers.[95] The temptation to become popular often stems from what Elder Robert D. Hales termed a teacher's desire to "be as an angel." Even with pure motives, however, if we hold up ourselves instead of the Savior, the result can be spiritually destructive rather than edifying:

> It is a great temptation to play the part of the Pied Piper and to figure that you are going to gather the youth

around you and love them into a testimony, or to feel
that if you can become very popular, you can lead and
be the role model and make a difference in the lives of
your youth.

While this may be true to a degree, there is nothing
more dangerous than when students turn their love and
attention to the teacher—the same way a convert sometimes does to a missionary—rather than to the Lord.
And then if the teacher or missionary leaves or conducts
his or her life contrary to the teachings of the gospel, the
students are devastated. Their testimonies falter. Their
faith is destroyed. The really great teacher is careful to
have the students turn themselves to the Lord.[96]

As President Howard W. Hunter cautioned teachers, we do not
need "personal disciples."[97]

But I thought you guys were all for making lessons interesting. Are you saying teachers shouldn't use humor or stories?

We're not opposed to using humor or stories occasionally to bring
doctrines and principles to life—but the motive has to be to better
illuminate the principle, not the teacher. As long as the motive is
pure, there's certainly a time and place for humor and stories and
even having a little fun with your students. For example, President
Hinckley uses humor very effectively. President Monson often
engages listeners with great stories.

There's definitely a balance to strike. There are two extremes to be
avoided: just playing games and entertaining, without any real
attempt to teach doctrine, on the one hand; or just lecturing on the
doctrine, without any real attempt to teach effectively, on the other.
Mark has seen some full-time gospel teachers who find themselves at
those extremes justify their approach by contrasting themselves with
people at the other extreme. Game players will say, "At least my
students are awake," as if that's the only way they could keep students
awake. And some lecturers will dismiss any attempt to introduce
variety into the classroom or to improve the quality of their teaching

as "gimmicks." It's as if they feel they are relieved from any obligation to improve their teaching by the fact that they teach doctrine.

Of course, balance doesn't mean a fifty-fifty split. It's more like the ratio of healthy food to dessert. If doctrine does not make up the bulk of the diet in our classes, our students will be spiritually malnourished. Elder Jeffrey R. Holland warned against that danger in these memorable terms:

> When crises come in our lives—and they will—the philosophies of men interlaced with a few scriptures and poems just won't do. Are we really nurturing our youth and our new members in a way that will sustain them when the stresses of life appear? Or are we giving them a kind of theological Twinkie—spiritually empty calories? President John Taylor once called such teaching "fried froth," the kind of thing you could eat all day and yet finish feeling totally unsatisfied.[98]

As between the two extremes, we'd much rather be guilty of teaching pure doctrine and being a little dry than of feeding our classes spiritual Twinkies. "I prefer doctrinal accuracy and spiritual certitude (even with a little dullness)," observed Elder Maxwell, "to charisma with unanchored cleverness."[99] Rob once knew missionaries who staved off boredom while tracting by playing a little game. Just before knocking on each door, one companion said an off-the-wall word like *bananas,* which the other companion then had to incorporate into his door approach. From the view of the guy behind the door, the message was probably rather baffling. From the missionaries' perspective, it was hilarious. They could barely wait until the door closed to start laughing.

But from heaven, the view had to be terribly disappointing. Who knows what work had been done on the other side of the veil to prepare this man for the day that the missionaries would knock on his door. And when the missionaries finally showed up, all they could say was, "Does life sometimes drive you bananas?" What seemed funny to the missionaries must have looked like a tragically squandered opportunity from a heavenly perspective.

Great gospel teachers realize that every class represents a sacred opportunity—a stewardship. If you prepare for every single lesson with that kind of attitude, you will go deeper and connect spiritually with students much more often than if you're just trying to get through the class. It's easy to underestimate students and teaching, whether we're teaching youth or adults. We may feel like spiritual experiences happen only on temple trips and at youth conferences. We may not have enough faith to believe they can happen in our Sunday School class or our early-morning seminary class or our elders quorum.

Nobody likes failure, either. Maybe one reason some teachers are more likely to play hangman than try to get students to share their testimonies about the Atonement is that they don't want to try to go deep and fail. You *know* you can get students to play hangman; it's safe, in a way. Trying to draw them out of their spiritual shells to get excited about the Atonement feels much riskier. But it's the adversary who wants us to feel that way. He wants us to play it safe, to keep Sunday School mundane, to underestimate our students' capacity for appreciating pure doctrinal truths. This is exactly what President J. Reuben Clark was talking about in "The Charted Course" when he said that the youth of the Church "are hungry for the things of the spirit; . . . they are eager to learn the Gospel, and they want it straight, undiluted. . . . You do not have to sneak up behind [them] and whisper religion in [their] ears; . . . you can bring these truths [out] openly."[100]

When we first heard this quote, we confess we wondered whether it really is true for the youth of our generation. But one of the things we've learned in years of teaching is that youth and even adult members are much more willing and even eager to drink from the fountain of pure doctrine than we ever would have suspected. That's not to say that if you do nothing but play games with a group of ninth graders that they'll complain. They probably won't. But if you tried doing that with students who have had a great gospel teacher for a year, they really would complain. Once they discover how satisfying the pure waters of the gospel are, students are no longer satisfied with fried froth and spiritual Twinkies.

- It's better to be appreciated in the long run than liked in the short run.
- Good teachers tell their students what they need to hear, not necessarily what they want to hear.
- Gospel teachers should hold up the Savior rather than themselves as the light.
- Your students need more than "fried froth" and games.

EIGHTEEN

SETTING THE STAGE
AND STAYING THE COURSE

The first few days of class present a unique opportunity and challenge for a teacher. Just as good employers tell their employees what to expect in advance—not after they mess up—good teachers set expectations for their students on the first day of class. Not only do they lay ground rules, but they also help students buy into the active approach to learning that we've discussed in this book—an approach that may well be quite a change for many of them. Because that approach will also be a change for many teachers, the first few days may also challenge the teacher's patience. Thus, the beginning of a new year or teaching experience is an important time for teachers to set the stage and stay the course.

I'm a little worried about the first day of class.

There's no need to be worried, but you should take it seriously. Just as the first five minutes of a lesson set the tone for the day, the first day or two of class set the tone for the entire year. And it's your best opportunity to set expectations for the class.

Like no chewing gum in class?

If you want to pick that particular battle, the first day would be the day to mention it. In a seminary setting, a lot of teachers like to really hammer home punctuality and order in the classroom on the first day, and it's certainly important to share any ground rules you have for the classroom. But if students come away from the first day of class feeling like the most important point was no chewing gum in class, an opportunity may have been missed. So while order in the classroom is important, it's probably better to emphasize what students can do to get the most out of class.

Many gospel students in the Church are accustomed to being passive students. For years they've sat back and just let the teachers talk—if they weren't busy heckling them. The great gospel teacher is aiming for something completely different. You want students to become active learners, and that requires them to approach the whole class differently. So you may as well tell them.

I thought I'm not supposed to lecture.

Good point, although lecturing is fine once in a while, just not as your dominant mode of teaching. But you're absolutely right—you'd really rather not begin the first day of class by lecturing. That's why we often start with this quote from Elder Eyring about attitude: "Rather than thinking, 'How good is he going to be today?' you could . . . say to yourself, 'What is it he is trying to accomplish?' Then you could ask yourself quietly, 'What can I do to help?' . . . That choice of an attitude will change the way you listen."[101] Then we ask a simple question: "So what are some of the things you can do to help make class better?" Or we ask, "What are some of the things you've done that have made some of your gospel classes better than others? How can you make a difference?" It's nothing brilliant, but it begins the process of helping them discover insights for themselves rather than just listening to a teacher spoon them out.

And what if they don't come up with all the things you want to cover?

It's no different than any other time you use discussion in teaching. Let them cover as many points as possible, building on them when appropriate. Then share any additional insights or cover any other principles the students haven't hit.

So what are the basic points you want to make sure to cover that first day?

This is a great time for a handout. In Mark's seminary classes, he calls it "Do Seminary." At the top is a quote from Elder Scott about the active role they need to play in the learning process: "Since the Lord will not force you to learn, you must exercise your agency to authorize the Spirit to teach you."[102] Then it lists five bullet points, most of them with supporting quotes.

What are the five points?

Read, listen, write, speak (meaning participate), and memorize. All of the supporting quotes come from Elder Scott's June 2002 *Ensign* article,[103] except for a quote about memorization that comes from his November 1999 *Ensign* article.[104]

That seems a little over the top for a Gospel Doctrine class.

It might be, but it's still worth discussing some of the principles from the handout, such as reading in advance and participating in class. It's your best chance to make a pitch for people to do the things that will really help them get the most out of any gospel class. And whether we're teaching youth or adults, it's best not to just establish expectations but to help the students understand the rationale behind the expectations. It's Theory Z.

Theory Z?

Theory Z was an approach to business management harnessing insights from the Japanese. A lot of top-down approaches to management relied heavily on punishments as negative incentives for performing, but Theory Z was a cooperative, open-book approach to running a company. Management listened to workers, and workers listened to management. In part, the idea was that workers who understood *why* management wanted them to do something performed tasks better than workers who were simply doing what they were told so they wouldn't get fired.[105]

It's a great philosophy when it comes to students—especially with participation. We could just insist they participate, but if they understand the benefits of participating, they're much more likely to participate. As mentioned in the chapter on shifting the burden to students, Rob starts his classes each semester by inviting students to talk about what they can do to get the most out of class—and he probably spends more time on participation than any other point. If he's feeling a little feisty, he might even ask them why teachers should let students participate at all, since teachers usually know more than their students. That usually sparks quite a discussion, and he draws out a lot of good comments about the benefits of participating. That's also a good time to challenge the naturally shy students to participate more than they usually do—and to let more talkative students know that they shouldn't be offended if you don't call on them every time they raise their hands.

That's me. In fact, the students may have to draw me out to get me to talk on the first day.

You'll be fine. As a matter of fact, one danger of reading a book like this one is that you might overanalyze yourself in the classroom. It's kind of like a golfer who tries to think about improving ten aspects of his swing while swinging. Sometimes you just need to stop thinking and step up and whack it. While you want to take the principles we've shared seriously, don't worry if you're not able to incorporate them all immediately. Just teach the best way you know how and work on being a little bit better each week. Focus on one thing at a time. Pick *Openers* or *questions* and focus on it for a while before adding *variety* or *journaling*.

Remember the early-morning seminary teacher who approached us at the in-service meeting and complimented us on our presentation on Openers, even as he admitted that he'd gone back to doing it the old way. That teacher was feeling what we all feel when we try to make significant changes in anything we do. The urge to just go back to what worked for us before is enormous. That's especially true with participation. When you're asking questions and getting nothing but blank stares, it's very tempting to revert to lecturing or telling a story. Implementing a change like that just takes time. Not only does the teacher need to master some new skills, but the class has to adjust to a new way of doing things. And at first, some of the students figure they can just ride out the silence. If they're silent long enough, they assume you'll finally give up and answer the question yourself.

And many teachers do. But if you stick with it, they'll finally get the message that you're serious about getting them to participate. And as you develop the skills necessary to draw them out in discussion, they'll also find the courage and skills necessary to participate. Once they finally get used to it, they'll prefer it, and you'll be able to spark a discussion with very little effort.

As you spend some time during the first day or two laying out your expectations and sharing the reasons behind those expectations, it will help get things off to a good start. That kind of groundwork then commits you and the students to staying the course of active learning that we've been describing throughout this book.

I'm keeping my fingers crossed, but I'm still not sure I believe.

Don't underestimate yourself or the students. The very fact that you've taken the time to read this book shows how serious you are about teaching this class as well as you can. That kind of commitment is not lost on the Lord. And ultimately, it's His classroom, not yours. As Elder Eyring said, if you're feeling inadequate, like you can't do this on your own, you're right.[106] Fortunately, you don't need to do it on your own. As you seek the Lord's help, He will bless you and your students beyond anything you might imagine.

- Remember that the first day of class can set the tone for the year.
- Use the first day to help students decide to become active learners.
- Help students understand your expectations—and the rationale behind them.
- Stay the course.
- Trust in the Lord—after all, you're on His errand.

NINETEEN
RECOMMENDED READING

We hope this book is a helpful resource, but it only supplements the resources and direction provided by those ordained to give us guidance. In this chapter we discuss several of the books, articles, and handbooks we have found most useful.

What are your favorite books on teaching?

The Book of Mormon, the Bible, the Doctrine and Covenants, and the Pearl of Great Price. The scriptures are full of what we should teach, along with great examples and insights on how we should teach. In addition to the standard works, two cornerstones of any gospel teacher's library should be President Packer's classic, *Teach Ye Diligently*, and the official manual from the Church, *Teaching, No Greater Call*. They both contain enduring principles and are well worth reading. Elder Jay E. Jensen believes that *Teaching, No Greater Call* is "one of the greatest publications on education on the face of the earth" and that "it is tremendously underused."[107]

How about talks? Which articles and talks by the Church leaders have most influenced you?

A great place to start is with Elder Dallin H. Oaks's October 1999 conference talk, "Gospel Teaching," in which Elder Oaks lays out a few fundamental principles of good gospel teaching with typical clarity.[108] In "'A Teacher Come from God,'" Elder Jeffrey R. Holland does a marvelous job of reminding gospel teachers of our obligation to nourish students with the word of God rather than merely entertain them with "fried froth."[109] Elder Henry B. Eyring also emphasizes the importance of teaching real doctrine in his 1999 talk entitled, "The Power of Teaching Doctrine."[110] Rounding out this group is Elder Eyring's powerful address to CES educators in 2001. In that talk, he encouraged gospel teachers to raise their sights because the "spiritual strength sufficient for our youth to stand firm just a few years ago will soon not be enough."[111]

When it comes to teaching tactics, two great resources on how and why to teach by the Spirit are Elder Oaks's "Teaching and Learning by the Spirit" in the March 1997 *Ensign*[112] and Elder Holland's article in the January 2003 *Ensign*.[113] We also highly recommend Virginia H. Pearce's 1996 talk about creating a safe and welcoming classroom environment.[114] For participation, there's nothing better than Elder Richard G. Scott's 2005 address to CES educators in which he said "a 'talking head' is the weakest form of class instruction."[115] And as we mentioned in our chapter on shifting the burden of learning to students, we believe that teachers for years to come will be gleaning insights from Elder Bednar's 2006 address to religious educators, "Seek Learning by Faith."[116]

Perhaps the definitive talk for gospel teachers is President J. Reuben Clark's "The Charted Course of the Church in Education," which was recently reprinted in the *Ensign*.[117] Another talk in that classic mode is Elder Bruce R. McConkie's "The Teacher's Divine Commission."[118] Finally, if you only had time to read one thing about teaching, we'd make it *Teaching the Gospel,* the handbook CES puts out for its teachers.[119]

The direction given in these talks and books from the Lord's anointed will be of more than passing interest to gospel teachers because these people represent the Lord rather than themselves. By paying attention to the instructions of living prophets and other Church leaders, we can better understand both what the Lord would have us teach and how He would have us teach it. Of course, the beauty of continuing revelation and inspired leaders is that as soon as this book goes to print, other Church leaders will provide even more timely counsel for teachers.

ENDNOTES

1. Dallin H. Oaks, "Gospel Teaching," *Ensign,* Nov. 1999, 78, quoting Gordon B. Hinckley, "How to Be a Teacher When Your Role as a Leader Requires You to Teach," General Authority Priesthood Board Meeting, 5 Feb. 1969.

2. Dilworth B. Parkinson, "Line upon Line," *BYU Magazine,* Summer 2004, 45.

3. See Tiger Woods, *How I Play Golf* (New York: Warner Books, 2001), 85.

4. Henry B. Eyring, "We Must Raise Our Sights," *Ensign,* Sept. 2004, 14.

5. Dallin H. Oaks, "Focus and Priorities," *Ensign,* May 2001, 83.

6. Ezra Taft Benson, "The Gospel Teacher and His Message," Address to Religious Educators, Temple Square Assembly Hall, 17 Sept. 1976, in Church Educational System, *Charge to Religious Educators,* 3rd ed. (Salt Lake City: The Church of Jesus Christ of Latter-day Saints, 1994), 13.

7. Richard Lloyd Anderson, in "Book Reviews," *BYU Studies,* vol. 9, no. 2 (Winter 1969), 229.

8. See Church Educational System, *Book of Mormon Student Manual: Religion 121 and 122* (Salt Lake City: The Church of Jesus Christ of Latter-day Saints, 1996), 5.

9. Dallin H. Oaks, "Teaching and Learning by the Spirit," *Ensign,* Mar. 1997, 8.

10. Oaks, "Teaching and Learning by the Spirit," 10.

11. Oaks, "Teaching and Learning by the Spirit," 10.

12. See The Church of Jesus Christ of Latter-day Saints, *New Testament Teacher Resource Manual* (Salt Lake City: The Church of Jesus Christ of Latter-day Saints, 2005), 2–3.

13. Richard G. Scott, "To Understand and Live Truth," Address to CES Religious Educators, 4 Feb. 2005, West Jordan, UT, 2.

14. Henry B. Eyring, Address to CES Religious Educators, 2 Feb. 1996.

15. Joseph Fielding Smith, *Doctrines of Salvation: Sermons and Writings of Joseph Fielding Smith,* comp. Bruce R. McConkie (Salt Lake City: Bookcraft, 1954), 1:44; emphasis added.

16. John Taylor, *The Gospel Kingdom,* sel. G. Homer Durham (Salt Lake City: Bookcraft, 1943), 78, quoted in Jeffrey R. Holland, "'A Teacher Come from God,'" *Ensign,* May 1998, 25, 26–27.

17. Jeffrey R. Holland. "Teaching, Preaching, Healing," *Ensign,* Jan. 2003, 41.

18. Howard W. Hunter, "Eternal Investments," Address to Religious Educators, Temple Square Assembly Hall, 10 Feb. 1989, in Church Educational System, *Charge to Religious Educators,* 74.

19. Gordon B. Hinckley, *Teachings of Gordon B. Hinckley* (Salt Lake City: Deseret Book, 1997), 619–20, quoted in Oaks, "Gospel Teaching," 80.

20. Bruce R. McConkie, *The Promised Messiah* (Salt Lake City: Deseret Book, 1978), 516, quoted in *Teaching, No Greater Call: A Resource Guide for Gospel Teaching* (Salt Lake City: The Church of Jesus Christ of Latter-day Saints, 1999), 43.

21. Oaks, "Gospel Teaching," 79.

22. Harold B. Lee, "Stand Ye in Holy Places," *Ensign,* July 1973, 123.

23. Benson, "The Gospel Teacher and His Message," 11.

24. David Whitmer described the incident in this way: "One morning when he was getting ready to continue the translation, something

went wrong about the house and he was put out about it. Something that Emma, his wife, had done. Oliver and I went upstairs and Joseph came up soon after to continue the translation but he could not do anything. He could not translate a single syllable. He went downstairs, out into the orchard, and made supplication to the Lord; was gone about an hour—came back to the house, and asked Emma's forgiveness and then came upstairs where we were and then the translation went on all right. He could do nothing save he was humble and faithful." (Quoted in B. H. Roberts, *A Comprehensive History of The Church of Jesus Christ of Latter-day Saints: Century 1* [Salt Lake City: Deseret News Press, 1930], 1:131.)

25. See David A. Bednar, "Seek Learning by Faith," Address to CES Religious Educators, 3 Feb. 2006, West Jordan, UT.

26. Jay E. Jensen, BYU—Idaho Faculty Meeting, Rexburg, ID, 19 Aug. 2005.

27. Bednar, "Seek Learning by Faith," 1.

28. Bednar, "Seek Learning by Faith," 1.

29. Bednar, "Seek Learning by Faith," 3.

30. Bednar, "Seek Learning by Faith," 4.

31. Virginia H. Pearce, "The Ordinary Classroom—a Powerful Place for Steady and Continued Growth," *Ensign,* Nov. 1996, 11–12.

32. Bednar, "Seek Learning by Faith," 5.

33. David A. Bednar, Question-and-answer session, 3 Feb. 2006, West Jordan, UT. "An answer given by another person usually is not remembered for very long, if remembered at all. But an answer we discover or obtain through the exercise of faith, typically, is retained for a lifetime" (Bednar, "Seek Learning by Faith," 5).

34. See Wilbert J. McKeachie, *McKeachie's Teaching Tips,* 11th ed. (Boston: Houghton Mifflin Company, 2002), 31; see also David W. Johnson, Roger T. Johnson, and Karl A. Smith, *Cooperative Learning: Increasing College Faculty Instructional Productivity* (Washington, DC: George Washington University, 1991).

35. Scott, "To Understand and Live Truth," 3.

36. Harold B. Lee, quoted in Melvin Leavitt, "Elder Robert L. Backman: Be Where the Lord Can Find You," *New Era,* May 1982, 13; emphasis added.

37. Bednar, "Seek Learning by Faith," 4.

38. Scott, "To Understand and Live Truth," 3.

39. Asahel D. Woodruff, *Teaching the Gospel,* 2nd ed. (Salt Lake City: Deseret Sunday School Union Board, 1961), 37, quoted in Church Educational System, *Teaching the Gospel: A Handbook for CES Teachers and Leaders* (Salt Lake City: The Church of Jesus Christ of Latter-day Saints, 1994), 14.

40. Charles W. Eliot, quoted in Derek Bok, *Our Underachieving Colleges: A Candid Look at How Much Students Learn and Why They Should Be Learning More* (Princeton, NJ: Princeton University Press, 2006), 123; emphasis added.

41. See David A. Sousa, *How the Brain Learns: A Classroom Teacher's Guide,* 2nd ed. (Thousand Oaks, CA: Corwin Press, 2001), 95.

42. Henry B. Eyring, *To Draw Closer to God: A Collection of Discourses* (Salt Lake City: Deseret Book, 1997), 20–21.

43. Bednar, "Seek Learning by Faith," 2.

44. Boyd K. Packer, "Do Not Fear," *Ensign,* May 2004, 77; see also Boyd K. Packer, "Washed Clean," *Ensign,* May 1997, 9; Boyd K. Packer, "Little Children," *Ensign,* Nov. 1986, 16.

45. Boyd K. Packer, quoted in Holland, "Teaching, Preaching, Healing," 37.

46. Dallin H. Oaks, "Following the Pioneers," *Ensign,* Nov. 1997, 72; emphasis in original.

47. Oaks, "Gospel Teaching," 80.

48. Dallin H. Oaks, "Resurrection," *Ensign,* May 2000, 14.

49. Oaks, "Gospel Teaching," 79.

50. Oaks, "Gospel Teaching," 80.

51. Scott, "To Understand and Live Truth," 2–3.

52. *Teachings of Presidents of the Church: Wilford Woodruff* (Salt Lake City: The Church of Jesus Christ of Latter-day Saints, 2005), vii, ix; see also *Teaching the Gospel*, 14.

53. "The Family: A Proclamation to the World," *Ensign*, Nov. 1995, 102.

54. For an excellent discussion of the importance of timing generally, see Dallin H. Oaks, "Timing," *Ensign*, Oct. 2003, 10–17.

55. President Packer endorses the idea of preparing each lesson by envisioning a student who asks, "So what?" and striving to make the doctrines relevant (see Boyd K. Packer, *Teach Ye Diligently* [Salt Lake City: Deseret Book, 1991], 143–45).

56. Scott, "To Understand and Live Truth," 3.

57. David A. Bednar, BYU—Idaho General Faculty Meeting, Rexburg, ID, 26 Aug. 2003.

58. Kim B. Clark, "My Grace Shall Attend You," Brigham Young University—Idaho Devotional, 7 June 2005 (http://www.byui.edu/Presentations/Transcripts/Devotionals/2005_06_07_ClarkKim.htm).

59. Scott, "To Understand and Live Truth," 2.

60. See Oaks, "Teaching and Learning by the Spirit," 8.

61. Scott, "To Understand and Live Truth," 3.

62. Pearce, "The Ordinary Classroom," 12–13.

63. See Robert G. Jones, "Asking Questions First," *Ensign*, Jan. 2002, 23–25.

64. See Russell G. Bulloch, "When Students Are the Teachers," *Ensign*, Jan. 2003, 17–19, for a good discussion of this and other similar techniques.

65. For a good discussion of how to increase participation in classes generally, see Jonn D. Claybaugh and Amber Barlow Dahl, "Increasing Participation in Lessons," *Ensign*, Mar. 2001, 33.

66. Neal A. Maxwell, "Teaching by the Spirit—'The Language of Inspiration,'" Address to Religious Educators, Brigham Young University, 13 Aug. 1991, in Church Educational System, *Charge to Religious Educators*, 60.

67. Robert D. Hales, "Teaching by Faith," *Ensign*, Sept. 2003, 22.

68. Brigham Young, quoted in Junius F. Wells, "Historic Sketch of the YMMIA: First Period," *Improvement Era*, June 1925, 715, quoted in Bednar, "Seek Learning by Faith," 5.

69. Boyd K. Packer, "The Candle of the Lord," *Ensign*, Jan. 1983, 51, 54–55; emphasis in original.

70. See Scott, "To Understand and Live Truth," 3.

71. Richard G. Scott, "Helping Others to Be Spiritually Led," Doctrine and Covenants and Church History Symposium, Provo, UT, 11 Aug. 1998. For an easily accessible but revised version of this talk, see Richard G. Scott, "To Acquire Knowledge and the Strength to Use It Wisely," *Ensign*, June 2002, 32–37.

72. Scott, "Helping Others to Be Spiritually Led," 1.

73. Scott, "To Acquire Knowledge," 32, 34; emphasis added.

74. Scott, "To Acquire Knowledge," 32.

75. Each of the testimonials in this chapter are actual quotes from Mark's students.

76. Teaching, *No Greater Call*, 98.

77. Neal A. Maxwell, "Start Making Chips," *New Era*, Sept. 1998, 4.

78. Neal A. Maxwell, "Those Seedling Saints Who Sit Before You," Address to Religious Educators, Brigham Young University, 19 Aug. 1983, in Church Educational System, *Charge to Religious Educators*, 34.

79. Scott, "To Understand and Live Truth," 3.

80. The Gospel Art Picture Kit is available online at www.lds.org by clicking on "Home & Family," then "Family Home Evening," and finally "Gospel Art Picture Kit."

81. Benson, "The Gospel Teacher and His Message," 15.

82. Joseph Smith, *Discourses of the Prophet Joseph Smith,* comp. Alma P. Burton (Salt Lake City: Deseret Book, 1977), 204.

83. For an interesting discussion on this subject, see Stephen E. Robinson, *Are Mormons Christians?* (Salt Lake City: Bookcraft, 1991), 13–18.

84. See, for example, Matthew 8:4; 17:9; Mark 7:36; 8:30; 9:9; and Luke 8:56.

85. Boyd K. Packer, "The Mantle Is Far, Far Greater Than the Intellect," Address to Religious Educators, Brigham Young University, 22 Aug. 1981, in Church Educational System, *Charge to Religious Educators,* 65; emphasis in original.

86. See http://www.truthorfiction.com/rumors/m/motherbird.htm. With convincing supporting details, this site contends that "both The National Geographic Society and officials at Yellowstone Park say [this story] never happened."

87. Jeffrey R. Holland, "A Prayer for the Children," *Ensign,* May 2003, 85–86.

88. Bruce R. McConkie, "The Teacher's Divine Commission," *Ensign,* April 1979, 21–22.

89. Hales, "Teaching by Faith," 22.

90. Hunter, "Eternal Investments," 75.

91. Packer, *Teach Ye Diligently,* 182.

92. Packer, *Teach Ye Diligently,* 157.

93. David O. McKay, *Man May Know for Himself: Teachings of President David O. McKay,* comp. Clare Middlemiss (Salt Lake City: Deseret Book, 1967), 340; emphasis in original.

94. Dallin H. Oaks, "Our Strengths Can Become Our Downfall," *Ensign,* Oct. 1994, 15.

95. Paul V. Johnson, "The Dangers of Priestcraft," CES Conference on the Doctrine and Covenants and Church History, Utah Valley State College, Orem, UT, 12 Aug. 2002.

96. Hales, "Teaching by Faith," 26.

97. Hunter, "Eternal Investments," 73.

98. Holland, "'A Teacher Come from God,'" 26–27, quoting Taylor, *The Gospel Kingdom,* 78.

99. Maxwell, "Teaching by the Spirit," 61.

100. J. Reuben Clark, "The Charted Course of the Church in Education," Address to Religious Educators, Brigham Young University Summer School at Aspen Grove, Utah, 8 Aug. 1938; 4, 9, quoted in Holland, "'A Teacher Come from God,'" 27.

101. Eyring, *To Draw Closer to God,* 20–21.

102. Scott, "To Acquire Knowledge," 34.

103. See Scott, "To Acquire Knowledge," 32–37.

104. See Richard G. Scott, "He Lives," *Ensign,* May 1999, 87–89.

105. See William G. Ouchi, *Theory Z* (Reading, MA: Addison-Wesley, 1981).

106. See Henry B. Eyring, "Rise to Your Call," *Ensign,* Nov. 2002, 75–76.

107. Jensen, BYU—Idaho Faculty Meeting, 19 Aug. 2005.

108. See Oaks, "Gospel Teaching," 78–80.

109. See Holland, "'A Teacher Come from God,'" 25–27.

110. See Henry B. Eyring, "The Power of Teaching Doctrine," *Ensign,* May 1999, 73–75.

111. See Eyring, "We Must Raise Our Sights," 14–19.

112. See Oaks, "Teaching and Learning by the Spirit," 7–14.

113. See Holland, "Teaching, Preaching, Healing," 32–43.

114. See Pearce, "The Ordinary Classroom," 11–12.

115. See Scott, "To Understand and Live Truth," 1–6.

116. See Bednar, "Seek Learning by Faith," 1–6.

117. See J. Reuben Clark, "Gospel Classics: Excerpts from The Charted Course of the Church in Education," *Ensign,* Sept. 2002, 55–61.

118. See McConkie, "The Teacher's Divine Commission," 21–24.

119. See *Teaching the Gospel.*

Rob Eaton

Rob Eaton received his bachelor's degree from BYU in international relations and his law degree from Stanford Law School. He practiced law for seven years in Seattle before becoming vice president of systems consolidation of The Regence Group for three years. In 2000 he left the legal and corporate world to teach institute and seminary full-time. He joined the Religious Education faculty at BYU—Idaho in June of 2004.

Mark Beecher

Mark Beecher graduated from BYU with his bachelor's degree in 1986 and received a Master's degree in social work from the University of Utah in 1994. He has been with the Church Educational System for twenty years now. He's also worked with Especially for Youth (EFY) since 1989 and has spoken to youth around the country. He is married to the former Kimberly Young. They have five children and currently reside in Saratoga Springs, Utah.